MOON DIVINATION
for Today's Woman

MOON DIVINATION
for Today's Woman

by

Cassandra Eason

foulsham

London•New•York•Toronto•Sydney

foulsham

Yeovil Road, Slough, Berkshire SL1 4JH

ISBN 0-572-01974-2

Printed in Great Britain by Cox and Wyman Ltd,
Reading, Berkshire.

Contents

Getting Back to
Moon Time

Lunatics, high and low tides, waxing, full and waning phases — what has the Moon got to do with the lives of modern women as they dash from office to supermarket to home? — apart from making them mutter: 'I must be loony to live like this'.

When you are vacuuming the carpet as the full moon rides it's hard to think of this as an offering of the fruits of your labour to the Moon Goddess Diana. Especially when Mr Free-Wheeler, who was going to take you round the world with only his guitar for baggage, turns out to have a mother and several aunties up for the day from Esher who are all coming to tea tomorrow.

Traditionally the Moon has been linked with women and the right-brain side of functioning, intuition, creative thinking and all those wonderful sources of wisdom and insight, the unconscious and superconscious that women have automatic access to. All that solar, logical, left-brain stuff actually gets in the way of women's natural radar sweep of the entire canvas of life. Most women can spot the missing piece while the guys are still unwrapping the jigsaw.

Moon divination which forms the basis of this book therefore taps, not into the solar outer cycle but the lunar pull of the inner woman. The planets we talk of reflect the mirror of the old alchemists, our inner stars. So you don't need to draw up birth charts or check the current position of the stars.

This inner lunar source of wisdom can be reached at any time, by using a simple moon cloth which we will make and planet stones: ordinary pebbles marked with basic symbols.

Magic?

Yes, because we cannot explain why time after time we choose stones that reflect our current dilemmas or why they fall in that area of the cloth where we have a stumbling block.

How does moon magic work? Who knows? But hundreds of women have used moon divination to home into the unconscious influences around them.

When we look at the physical Moon we see only the external form. The Moon has no natural light of its own and shines only by reflected sunlight. The physical moon is a desolate hostile world of rocks, mountains, some higher than Everest, and huge craters.

It is about 386,000 km (or 241,250 miles) away from Earth and takes just over 27 days to complete its orbit. The Moon influences the tides. We can expect very high and low tides at New and Full Moon and not nearly such extreme tides at the first and last quarter.

Even here we are aware of its influence on our inner world. For if the Moon rules the tides, it is not surprising she has a powerful influence over us.

How can we flow with the tides?

Indeed it has been recorded that fatal traffic accidents and suicides do increase when the Moon is full, as do violence and admissions for psychiatric treatment (the old term lunatic was coined because mentally unstable people became observably more so at the Full Moon).

One modern theory suggests that the Moon alters our internal chemistry by exerting a gravitational pull on our body fluids.

Another theory is that altered gravitational fields brought about by a full moon, cause electrically-charged particles to fall to Earth. These lead to changes in brain chemicals that make us feel ratty and blue. Men, as well as women, may find that organising their lives around the lunar monthly time span and daily tides, may put them in touch with apparently random mood changes. But it is women that seem especially vulnerable to the changes in the Moon.

What is more, the female menstrual cycle is on average 29.5 days which is also the time between two full moons. The average length of pregnancy is 266 days, which is the average number of days between 10 full moons. So women are very lunar oriented, especially during their fertile years.

These links have been acknowledged from the Dawn of Time. To the earliest tribes the Sun, Moon and stars were central to their existence and in cave paintings world-wide the moon goddess is shown in full pregnant glory.

Legends of the Moon Goddess

The influence of the Moon Goddess has been universal. The original Great Yang and Yin were the Sun and Moon. And the Indian subtle body has two snake-like conduits for the inner power called *Kundalini,* to rise within, the left for the Sun and the right for the Moon.

The first official Moon cult was founded in Greece in 500BC. The Moon was worshipped in her three aspects: the Maiden or Waxing Moon, the Mother or Full Moon and the Wise Woman or Crone, as the Waning and Dark of the Moon. Artemis, whose silver bow stood for the new moon, was in Ancient Greece, the goddess of the Waxing Moon. In Egypt, Isis the great mother, was worshipped as the fullness of the Moon, while Hecate represented its waning aspect to the Ancient Greeks. The Semitic Lilith became the Dark of the Moon. These are but a few examples of the universal theme.

Legends abound of Moon magic. It was believed that the souls of those who died were taken back into the Moon to be reborn and that each night the Moon gathered unwanted memories and forgotten dreams to fall as dew at dawn. Lakes are often called Diana's mirror. Above all, the Moon is regarded as the White Goddess, bringing inspiration to writers, poets and artists.

But this book is not going to ask you to bow down before the White Goddess, or any of the other gods and goddesses of ancient lore which are mentioned.

What we are going to do is to use them as convenient symbols, a sort of shorthand, for aspects of our life in much the same way that we talk about a person being mercurial (because they change quickly like Mercury, the fleet-footed messenger of the Gods) or being martial (like Mars the god of war).

Thinking in symbols

The moon symbols are particularly relevant to women because, even today, the triple aspect of the moon corresponds with the female growth cycle.

We set out when we leave school with our belief in equal rights that lasts until we're asked to put on the kettle for the guys, our first day at work. And find out that the boss's idea of filling us in on the job involves a trip to a sleazy wine bar after work to discuss his wife, 'who doesn't understand the pressures of executive life'.

Then there's mothering, the middle stage when biological mother or not, you can end up nurturing your partner and the elderly neighbours. At the same time as being an agony aunt to the office. As well as holding down a full-time job and trying to find a little bit that's still you.

As for the wise woman — most of us who are over forty would go straight for the crone label (where did the golden hours you were promised go?). Even if you made it in the marriage stakes all the way to the engraved silver teapot, there are grandchildren to babysit for, elderly relatives to placate or nurse and all those dreams still receding into a tomorrow that never comes.

Problems of living the solar way

Or you may be alone, struggling to hold down a job, pay the mortgage, put out the rubbish, mend the leaking loo and get through Sundays when the rest of the world goes past two by two, like Noah's Ark. At such times you may well wonder what happened to the fulfillment that the passing years were supposed to bring.

It's hard enough when we accept the natural

lunar cycle of female life with its tidal ebbs and flows of energy. But when we try to live the solar way instead, the A to Z linear dash, we end up ratty, unfulfilled and accused of being hormonal, when we are simply not tuned into an alien life pattern.

What is more, these lunar cycles recur in our monthly and even daily lives. There are times when we are full of enthusiasm and eager to put in the groundwork, write those letters or go out and try new activities and are receptive to new people and influences. These are the good days, when we can go for that change, juggle work and home and end up whistling and singing.

But days or hours later, here we are gnawing our way through the biscuit tin to gain the energy we haven't got, instead of reflecting and letting the world go by.

And so Moon divination is relevant to women of all ages and stages. Whether you look at your lives on a daily or monthly basis, or at the wider ebbs and flows of your life cycle. And the last part of the book discusses practical ways of living by the moon, without needing to display your wobbly bits and cavort in the woods.

After a week of using this book you'll be doing your own readings. And after six weeks or so you'll have modified the system so much in the light of your unique needs — and even more special intuitions — that you'll hardly recognise my basic formula. All my books are written for the best clairvoyant of all: you. Whatever system you use, or even if you use all of them at different times, you'll be in charge of your own destiny. Moon Magic is special because it puts us in touch with the part of ourselves that links with women in times past. Hundreds of years on, women will still have the same problems with relationships and trying to find a place for themselves but will still look up at the moon. (Women of the future may even travel there — though no doubt they'll be left struggling with the moon buggy full of shopping and space tots.)

The message will always be the same: trust yourself and those inner rhythms that link you with nature. We are all special and magical, though sometimes it's hard to remember. If in doubt, look at the world by moonlight when it is more mystical.

And don't forget your lunar magic that has been there for women of all times and is there for you.

Happy Moonday!

Moon Workings

The idea of moon workings at first sounds very mysterious but like the rest of the system it's remarkably down to earth and cheap. Before we can start doing all this moon magic we need some basic items.

You may like to choose a special day to collect what you will need and make the first steps to getting off the frantic solar race-track. In an ideal world you'd pick the day of the new moon and get up early when the dew is on the grass (remember that some legends tell us that the dew is the Moon's way of recycling all the discarded dreams and memories).

Gathering your moon materials

You'll make this day yours to be alone and choose your treasures. You might, perhaps, take a bus or train ride into a town you've always wanted to visit and finish up with tea and some calorie-laden delicacy.

Once you are in tune with yourself, your inner beauty will shine through and people will think you've lost weight, had a new hair-do or got a new man and you won't constantly feel the need to deprive your body of food to satisfy someone else's idea of desirability. Then you'll be home in time for a nice long soak in jasmine (a moon fragrance), or other scented bath oil. Put a pinkish or golden light bulb in the bathroom and watch your sags, bumps and bags become the sensuous shape of a woman of mystery (well we can dream!!)

You will need:

1. The Stones.

If you've got a pebbly garden, then it would be a very special experience to collect your stones by moonlight. But for those of us who need to go to beach, park, gravel pit or recreation ground, early morning is better. The pale moon may still be in the sky and you're less likely to be set on by the local lads, or have the neighbours muttering about 'that funny woman at number 9 cavorting in the moonlight!'

Collect sixteen stones of any colour so long as they are similar with a flat surface to draw on. They should be slightly bigger than a 2p coin.

2. A Moon Diary

You can keep all kinds of information about your daily and monthly highs and lows as your moon workings progress. But at first we'll just record the moon readings, so that you can look back on each of them and see how your life evolves once you understand the underlying currents. You don't need an expensive diary.

Any notebook will do as you'll be calling the days 1 to 28 (for each lunar month).

Make sure you choose one you like (mine's got a silver sheen cover because it reminded me of the moon and it was in the reduced rack). Then you will feel it's a part of you. Most newspapers have a moon of the day picture under the weather section, which you can either copy at the top of the relevant page or cut out and stick in with the calendar date each day just for reference.

3. A drawstring bag or pouch.
Buy or make a little drawstring bag, pouch or purse to keep your stones, not away from the light according to ancient superstition, but safe and a part of you and not for the world to poke and exclaim over. For moon magic is essentially private, a marking of your unique identity (though when you are confident, you might like to share your readings with a friend and perhaps come together at the New Moon to light candles).

4. A piece of cloth
Any remnant will do as long as it is at least a foot square. Just buy one for a few pence if you have nothing suitable around. Any colour will do as long as the stones show up. Old plain scarves make excellent cloths.

5. A permanent marker
This can be in black, gold or silver (the colour of the moon) or acrylic paint to draw the signs

17

on your stones. You may like to use a silver marker for drawing the cloth too. It's always useful for designing an urgent birthday card or gift tag, so your money won't be wasted.

6. A silver candle (optional).

After your busy and, I hope, happy day, you can light your candle, ring it with your stones and sit quietly in the darkness and let the world go away.

If it's warm, sit in your garden and perhaps the new moon will shine down on you and remind you that it is possible to start again. Although it may take many new moons before you can begin to see your path — and perhaps many setbacks. For each new moon promises hope and a fresh start. It's never too late.

We're not practising any weird ritual, just tuning into our natural magic and recognising that the moon that controls the tides of the earth, shines over sea and city high rise flat alike, and that all women are very special creatures. Or you might like to leave your stones in the new moonlight and make a wish, as you did when you were a child, turning over a piece of silver or a silvery coin.

Once back indoors, write your wish on a piece of paper, burn it in the candle flame and watch the smoke carry your hopes to the cosmos. Then blow out your candle and send the light to yourself and remember that you are as deserving of love as anyone else.

All this sounds ideal. But maybe the new moon is skulking behind a cloud. Or perhaps you have bought this book when the moon is just beginning to wane and you want to start right now. If so, just copy or stick the current moon picture from your morning paper as Day One.

You can always start on a Monday, the day sacred to the Moon (but don't be put off from starting now if it's Wednesday. You are the one who makes a day special. It need not be the other way round).

The magic is in you, not some external ritual and should be your servant, not your mistress.

Don't worry if, instead of the lovely leisurely day browsing round the gift shops of the local olde worlde town and searching for just the right piece of cloth (in between tea shops) you have to cram your moon shopping along with a visit to the supermarket for cat litter and washing powder, or between work and picking up the children from the childminder.

Don't fret if the kids bang on your door demanding loo paper or telling you the cat's been sick while you're trying to be alone and spiritual. Or your flatmates insist on intruding on your inner silence with their Heavy Metal music.

Have a giggle — magic, like the rest of your life, is going to have to be on the run. Accept

19

that. Go with the flow. Each moment you snatch back from the world is a victory. Your inner strength and peace will grow as you etch back your unique outline (sags, bags and all) instead of wondering if you even exist.

Start from where you are and not where you would like to be. Stop just for a second to look at the moon (or imagine it behind a cloud) and, remembering all the women down the ages who have snatched odd moments for the important things, know you are very special.

Moon magic operates in space and silence and if yours, like mine, has been eroded over the years, it's essential to start claiming it back inch by inch.

Each day, you will mark on a stone the sign of a planet or element in permanent marker, silver or black acrylic paint and then put it in your bag.

When you've made the first six stones, you can make the cloth.

The design is not at all complicated, just three circles to reflect the three stages of female inner life and outside the quarters of the solar seasons, spring, summer, autumn and winter.

After all we've got to live in a man's world and it can be useful to see your life against the wider sweep.

The Planet Stones

You will only mark one side of your Planet Stones. But if you throw your stone face down, it is as significant as if your stone lands marked side up.

Day 2

The first of the Planet Stones

Turn it over very gently and see what it is you are holding back.

Women often deny both their strengths and true feelings, either for fear of hurting others, or because we don't feel we have any right to negative thoughts. Nice girls don't boast, push to the front of the queue of life, or otherwise draw attention to themselves (remember what you were told in Brownies).

So when the going gets rough and you are having to fight for promotion or recognition — suddenly you hear Mum or Brown Owl reminding you of your manners.

When you do get the blank face of your planet stones uppermost, ask yourself why you need to avoid an issue. The answer may give you a vital clue to your destiny.

The Three Planet Stones of Decision

The Sun: This is simply a circle with a dot in the middle. Draw or paint the sign on your first pebble. If you think of the dot as the seed or potential for personal achievement then you won't go far wrong.

All cultures have worshipped the Sun. In Ancient Greece, the solar God, Helios, was praised each dawn as he emerged in the East and drove his chariot of winged horses around the sky. Sun deities on a whole are male and the Sun's metal is gold.

Of course women too have got this lovely competitive solar oomph in them and letting our energies develop is vital if we are to make our place in the sun. The only problem comes when we live entirely the solar way and deny our intuitive moon side. But in right measure it is as vital as the caring side of men.

If you get the **Sun Stone** in a reading, then you may be faced with a new opportunity or direction. But you are scared because you know that it means showing and developing your strengths, even if this means treading on a few toes.

Yet this can be far more exciting than sitting on the sidelines of life and even if the chance presented is not what you had planned, it may well be a vital step forward. Many a would-be novelist ends up writing trade manuals and getting great satisfaction both materially and creatively. It's those people who won't change direction and stick rigidly to outworn life-plans based on, Enid Blyton or Barbara Cartland, who find their energies dammed up in resentments or regrets. So go for it.

When the **Sun** is hidden, you may be encouraging those closest to you to live out your dreams and getting angry when they fail. If you wanted to be a teacher but never were and eldest daughter is set on taking up decorating or plumbing, don't try to divert her down the path you never took.

We've all got our own destinies and it's never too late to train or retrain and reach the goal yourself. On the other hand, when you take charge of your own potential, you may find your ambitions have changed and you want to take up plumbing or hang-gliding after all!

Day 3

The Moon: Depending on how it falls, this stone can look like the new moon, the waning moon or a crescent lying on its back or front. But whichever way it falls, you will know that it is talking about the inner you.

The Moon has traditionally been regarded as the consort of the Sun, her silver to his gold, the Queen Luna to his King Sol in alchemy.

But the Moon is far more than this. The **Moon Stone** represents feminine power — the deep, unconscious, intuitive gifts that are especially

The Moon

highly developed, or perhaps least repressed in women. The Roman Diana (sister of the Sun God, Apollo) is often taken as the Moon in all her aspects. The Moon offers an alternative perspective. Look at any scene with its man-made categories in the harsh light of day. Then see the same scene without artificial light, with only the lunar glow. The apparent certainties fade and what we dismissed as without foundation becomes possible and indeed the only course. The measurable world is only a half and perhaps the tip of the iceberg.

If you get the **Moon,** then you are overdosing on logic and other people's advice. Whether the decision is major or minor, at work or at home, refuse to be pressurised into an instant decision — that's solar stuff. Step back into yourself and listen to your inner voice. You can find the answer to your dilemma within you, if only you can clear your space from other people's clutter and use your inner wisdom.

When your **Moon** sign is hidden you may be feeling a bit low on inspiration and tempted to take the line of the least resistance. This is the negative side of the moon when it seems easier to accept that your partner/boss/mum/the expensive clairvoyant at the end of the pier — or even the lady who brings the tea trolley round at work probably does know best. But then you are handing over your future to others to make and in the long run that can only bring pain. Don't kid yourself. Listen to your dreams and day-time visions.

Day 4

The Earth

The Earth: You can draw or paint the earth stone as a circle with an X touching the edges. This planet very rarely appears in astrology because it's where we are and we can feel it beneath our feet. So where's the magic? But as any amateur quantum physicist you meet in the supermarket check-out queue or the saloon bar at the Flying Horse will tell you, there's no such thing as an objective viewpoint: the perceiver affects what is perceived.

And as for Earth magic: what about those crystals, the Standing Stones, the leys of power, the flowers and the trees? And most important of all, remember Demeter the Earth Goddess with her sheaves of corn. Without her harvests man would starve. We connect to earth magic with the soles of our feet and our five senses; the Earth isn't just a backdrop to the real play. Have you seen the pictures of the beautiful blue earth taken from the Moon?

We are creatures of the Earth as much as the spirit and we ignore at our peril the information pouring in through our senses, especially our common sense that reminds us of our priorities and the realities.

If you get the **Earth Stone**, then you may be ignoring the information that is staring you in the eye and allowing your common sense to be blinded by science or what other people, especially those in authority, tell you are the facts.

Start with what you see and hear for yourself

and use your innate common sense to separate the jargon from the trees.

When the **Earth Stone** is hidden you may be feeling out of touch with the real world. Sort out who and what really matter to you and value those who offer you real friendship or love, even if they aren't as exciting as fair-weather friends.

A Planet Stones reading

A Reading of Three Planet Stones

We now have three stones marked out. What can we do with them? At this stage, if you try a reading it cannot be a representative one. But it's no bad idea, even with just three stones, to pull a stone out every day and see if it has any bearing on what is happening in your life.

You may get the same stone three days running, in which case it is obviously a key issue. But to give you an idea how the system works, we shall eavesdrop on a real reading, in which the three stones we have marked cropped up when Helen made a daily selection over three days using a full set.

Helen's reading

Helen is in her forties and has one son Luke who is four. Luke is a very intelligent child and sometimes finds it difficult to talk to children of his own age.

Recently he started nursery school but Helen has been told by the teacher who has just left

college, that Luke is maladjusted because he
prefers to read and draw rather than join in the
rough and tumble with the other children. The
teacher is behaving in a very negative way
towards Luke and has suggested that he will
never fit in with school life. Helen is devas-
tated, especially as the Head Teacher says that
it is not her policy to go against the assessment
of her staff . Helen draws.

Day 1. **The Sun.** ☉

Day 2. **The Earth.** ⊗

Day 3. **The Moon.** ☽

There is no contradiction since the stones are
suggesting she calls into play all her powers.
First is her solar energy, the determination to
insist that her child is valued for what he is and
not condemned because he does not fit the pre-
determined mould of an inexperienced teacher.
The **Sun** reminds us of our own abilities: as a
mother, Helen knows her child's behaviour
patterns better than anyone. But sometimes it
is hard to have the confidence to assert our
valid opinions. Helen is an intelligent woman
and should not be intimidated by someone
hiding behind the role of 'a professional'.

If necessary, Helen may have to consider
either finding another school for her child, or

going beyond the apathetic Head Teacher to insist that her child is not unfairly labelled.

The **Earth Stone** reminds Helen to trust her common sense and not allow jargon to blind her to what she knows: that her child is just very intelligent and needs stimulating. It is easy to be panicked by the condemnation of so-called experts and if she talks to other parents she may find they too have had problems with this teacher. There is the often-quoted and quite true example of a teacher who wanted a child assessed because she always drew in black crayon. The psychologist called in to study the child's morbid tendencies, pointed out that she had lost all the other colours in her tin but was too scared to say so.

The **Moon Stone** assures Helen that she instinctively knows her child better than anyone and that if she 'feels' the environment is wrong for him, then she should follow her instincts and not be pressured to accept what others tell her. It is hard to go against the way things are but sometimes it is important to avoid future pain. Our instinctive knowledge, the lunar aspect, is as valuable as the solar, conscious understanding.

Helen has an excellent trio of conscious, unconscious and common-sense wisdom to see that her son gets the best deal. Often the needs of bright children are overlooked and teachers appear to be only too eager to brand a clever child disruptive, when the failings lie in their own inability to stimulate children who operate at a higher level.

Mercury, the fourth Planet Stone, represents the Roman winged messenger of the gods (known as Hermes to the Greeks) who was the son of Jupiter. Carrying a rod entwined with two serpents that could induce sleep, he winged his way between the heavens, earth and underworld in his role as celestial postman.

Through his skill and dexterity (and even his thieving ways), he came to rule over commerce and medicine (like Hermes his Greek counterpart). A very versatile chap. **Mercury** is also the smallest planet and the nearest to the sun, whizzing round the sun in just 88 days. But he's obviously not a planet to meet if you fancy a gentle meander among the rose bushes.

Mercury

Drawing **Mercury** is very easy: a half circle pointing upwards — the container for inspiration — with a circle underneath and a cross under that. The circle represents the spirit and the cross represents matter.

In our system, **Mercury** is all about messages and communication. And with all that flying about from sphere to sphere there is bound to be the odd crossed wire.

Communication is our greatest gift, whether verbal or non-verbal (even the odd missile can convey our feelings or intent), by letter, fax, telephone or even Interflora.

Communication at its best can bring us close to people, iron out misunderstandings and convey what it is we want and what we are prepare to give. Winston Churchill's 'Jaw, jaw not war, war' should sum up **Mercury**. So, on the face of it, we should be pretty pleased when he appears.

But, in real life, communication is not so simple. What we say is rarely what we mean and what we ask for may not be what we want or need. The simplest remark can be so loaded that we can end up in full-blown conflict.

Take a typical scenario: Mr Free-Wheeler and Ms Executive have been sharing a flat in what passes for reasonable bliss till his mother announces she's coming to tea.

Mr Free-Wheeler thinks: 'Oh God, my mother's coming to inspect me and as soon as she sets foot over the door I'll be wrong as usual. Wrong girl, tatty flat, no career prospects. A "kept man", she calls me. I've never been able to please her — unlike my perfect accountant brother with his detached house in Esher, 2.4 children and his ghastly, houseproud wife. I'd hate to live like them.

'But she'll tell Liz what I'm really like and there goes another relationship. She is my mother. She must be right. I'll have to tidy up, repaint. Oh God.'

So he says: 'My mother's coming to tea, the flat's a mess and mum's very particular.'

Ms Successful Executive hears the underlying message: 'You're a slut! You don't look after me properly. Real women look after their men and keep their houses neat and tidy like my wonderful sister-in-law.'

She thinks: 'That's what my mother says. "No wonder nobody will marry you. I'll never have grandchildren and it's your fault. Real women stay at home and have babies. And why can't you get a man who can support you?"

'I don't want to stay at home and cook and clean and have children, I like living this way. But Mum must be right.'

Then Ms Executive says: 'Not good enough for you, hey? If you earned a decent salary we'd be able to pay a cleaner or I could stay home and be like your precious sister-in-law and iron your shirts.'

Mr Free-Wheeler says: 'So you wanted a meal ticket? Shame you didn't marry that smarmy b****** from accounts. And at least my brother can find a clean shirt.'

And so it goes on, with both sides talking but neither really listening. Instead the unspoken words in their heads are carrying the day.

If you get **Mercury** in a reading, then communication is the central issue. There's something you need to say. But it's important to be sure you express your needs or opinions clearly and without emotion or back-biting and that you listen to what the other person is really saying in return. You may find you are on the same wavelength once the chaff and resentments are cleared out of the way.

When **Mercury** is hidden, then most of the communication is taking place in your head — probably in the middle of the night and you are taking both parts in the argument and coming out worst.

Don't anticipate defeat, or, worse still, be so exhausted or dispirited with the inner rehearsal that you don't bother.

Day 7

Venus

Venus is sometimes known as the Morning or Evening Star, because she shines with brilliant silvery hue. At her peak, she is the brightest object in the sky apart from the Sun and Moon. She is also the closest planet to Earth and the closest in size. For this reason she is sometimes regarded as Earth's twin although, in fact, Mars is more like Earth.

And of course, **Venus**, as every romantic knows, is the Goddess associated with love and beauty and daughter of Jupiter.

But it wasn't all roses for her. Her celestial dad married her off to her half-brother Vulcan, God of the Forge and one of the less prepossessing gods, in return for some thunderbolts, and she had to set up home inside a volcano.

This sign is simple to draw: a circle with a cross underneath (used to represent the female in biology).

But Venusian type encounters are few and far between on the 5.16 to Penge and so **Venus** also addresses the issue of all our relationships of the heart, from great-gran to best friend.

For we don't live on a desert island with our twin soul, assuming we meet one without 2.4 existing children and a hefty maintenance bill. And relationships past as well as present can affect our present reactions, as we saw with **Mercury**.

If you have been hurt in an affair of the heart it is all too easy to be too suspicious of your new lover. He may do something quite innocently but the thought flashes into your head: 'That's just what Roger used to say when he was sneaking off to see that slut from the bank.' Then, before you can stop yourself, you are transferring all the old grievances to the new man in your life.

This scenario applies equally to friends and even relatives.

If you get **Venus** in a reading, then relation-ships are the name of the game and the loving feelings may be a bit thin on the ground. You may find yourself trying to keep the happy family ship afloat or placate your flatmates or best friend. But sometimes we can try too hard

and see our lives purely in terms of our relationships with others. You can forget that you are
a person with your own very set likes and
dislikes and find yourself going along with the
flow for the sake of peace and quiet.

Although it may give you peace and quiet in
the short term, in the long term, easy and
mutually satisfying interactions are less likely
if we are providing 90 per cent of the input (99
per cent if you are dealing with a teenage
child).

So if you can feel that bright smile lighting up
your face and it doesn't reach your eyes, back
off and let others take their share of responsibility for good relations.

If **Venus** is hidden, then you may be looking
at people in terms of the roles they occupy and
not whether you like them or approve of their
actions. This can lead to both false expecta-
tions and guilts.

If sister or daughter is being a pain, then you
shouldn't be expected to accept unfair treatment just because you are mum or little sister.

Often the roles are set early and we end up
spending time with relations whom we don't
really like and who maybe are also only seeing
us out of duty and ending up feeling resentful
on both sides.

So feel free to ease up on this role.

Mars is the planet with a reddish tinge. Red being seen as a warlike colour, it ended up with the name of the Roman God of War. It takes 687 days to orbit the Sun and is almost half the size of Earth. It is drawn as a circle with an arrow at 45 degrees on top (used in biology to represent the male) and it is a very masculine planet.

Mars, son of Jupiter, was the father of Romulus and Remus who founded Rome. As God of both agriculture and war, he very much represented the ideal Roman, first as farmer and then as conqueror.

Mars

His mother, Juno, said she gave birth to him by means of union with a fabulous flower — but I don't recommend trying out this excuse on today's husbands after an extra-marital fling!

In our system **Mars**, the angry planet, represents the negative side of ourselves that we deny or foist on to others because, especially for women, anger, resentment and the rest are not emotions we are encouraged to acknowledledge.

Yet without anger and resentment change wouldn't come about. You keep plodding round the old treadmill, swallowing the same petty injustices, day after day, week after week, until — suddenly — enough is enough and you find yourself saying so. Then you're into a new ball game. The association of **Mars** with anger and war isn't a bad one unless we turn the anger on ourselves, or end up lashing out blindly at the nearest and usually wrong target. Save your anger for the petty official and not for your partner or your children (unless they really deserve it).

Often we do need the iron of **Mars** (its natural metal according to the old alchemists) to make others realise that we do have needs and rights.

If you get **Mars** in a reading, you are probably feeling flaming mad, or at least pretty resentful about the way things are. So it's time to state quite clearly your grievances — but not to a long-suffering partner or friend who can only be sympathetic but cannot change things. Go straight to the top and go for the jugular!

Sometimes it's so difficult for women to protest that, when they finally get round to it, they are so seething that their carefully thought out arguments end as an incoherent boiling mass.

You end up in tears with the real injustice unsolved and the perpetrator smelling of roses as usual. So attack before you reach boiling point and go for it logically and with determination.

There are times when you have got to tread on a few toes if your feelings aren't to be trampled on or eroded. If **Mars** is hidden, then you are probably using a lot of energy keeping the lid on your feelings. You have constant headache or backache from keeping your muscles tensed for action. You are eating too much, drinking too much or smoking too much.

Wonder creams won't get rid of crows' feet. What will really help you is stopping the twenty-four-hours-a-day smile that you keep firmly fixed on your face when you feel like yelling. So let **Mars** out of the closet and let rip.

Day 9

A reading for Meg
Six Planet Stones down and six to go. The next stage is to make our Moon Cloth to cast them on. But before we do that, let's eavesdrop on someone else's reading over three days.

A reading with three stones

As before, I have chosen a case in which the subject picked at random from a full set of Moon Stones but selected three which we have already come across.

Meg is in her seventies and feels that she's lost control of her life since her husband died and she moved in with her daughter. Although she is getting progressively deafer, Meg is otherwise as fit and alert as ever.

But she finds that the world in general, and her daughter in particular, act as if she is senile — although all she really needs is for people to face her and speak clearly. For her, the last straw came when her daughter and the optician discussed whether she should have bifocals or two sets of glasses without involving her in the conversation at all.

Her daughter is hinting that Meg should go along to the senior citizens' club at the local day centre. But Meg is raring to join the University of the Third Age.

Meg's Reading

From her complete set of the twelve stones, Meg draws:

Day 1: **Mars**

Day 2: **Venus**.

Day 3: **Mercury**.

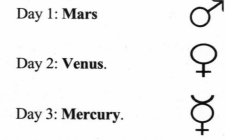

Mars mirrors Meg's frustrations at being treated as though she is over the hill. This is made worse by her hearing problems and Meg knows that before long she is going to flip, which will confirm her daughter's view that her mother has become just a dotty old woman.

So the time has come for Meg to put her foot down and insist that her daughter stops acting as interpreter to the world and lets her speak for herself.

Meg needs independence. If she can get transport to the senior citizens's club, she can probably arrange it to the local College of Education, where there will be facilities for hard of hearing students of all ages.

Venus highlights a central issue. The relationship has changed radically now that Meg's daughter has assumed the mothering role and is steamrolling her way through what she sees as her duties to her ailing mother, regardless of her mother's real needs.

So it's high time that Meg did a little redefining and asserted herself as a person, and not just as 'poor old mum'.

This will probably come as quite a shock to her daughter who has quickly become used to her new role. But ultimately it may prove a relief to both sides since they will be able to relate as individuals and not through pre-assigned roles.

Mercury is the stone of communication and Meg's hearing disability obviously puts obstacles in the path of clear communication. It is a sad fact that any form of disability tends to be regarded as symptomatic of mental feebleness (It's known, and hated, as the 'Does she take sugar' syndrome). There are people with PhDs in wheelchairs who get treated like five-year-olds.

So it does take a lot of courage, especially when coming up against professionals who may not always be especially sensitive, to explain how they can help you to understand clearly what they are saying and if necessary stop them for clarification. Equally, it's important for Meg to convey to her daughter, not resentment, but practical suggestions as to how she can help her mother to have her needs recognised.

This is how the reading worked for Meg, but think of it only as an example rather than a set rule when you read for yourself.

Keep drawing a stone from your bag each morning, if possible, to highlight the key issue of the day that has been working its way through your dreams and half-waking states throughout the night.

If the same stone appears again and again, then it may well be highlighting something vital that you are avoiding. Take some time to think, not only about this hidden issue, but also about those reasons that are making you, probably unconsciously, push it to the back of your mind.

Note your daily readings down in your moon diary, together with your drawn moon phase, and you may find that certain issues are repeated in a monthly cycle. You can either adjust yourself to this cycle or make plans to break away from it. Either way, you must use the Planet Stones to take charge of your own destiny, not to foretell it.

Making the Moon Cloth

Our first readings have been based on choosing Planet Stones at random and thinking about them. But the Stones can also be cast on to a cloth divided in to sections and we can read their meanings in conjunction with where they fall. Any piece of fabric between 12 and 15 inches square will do for a Moon Cloth (perhaps an old scarf). Use whatever colour you feel is suitable so long as the stones will show up well on it when thrown (it's best to avoid intricately patterned cloth).

You can mark it in any indelible marker or paint stick in silver, the moon's colour, black or dark blue. The solar bits can be drawn in gold (the sun's colour) if you like, but I prefer my cloths to be just one colour.

One word of warning: unless you fancy redecorating, don't leave your indelible paint stick or marker where a toddler can reach it. Mine did a beautiful Moon design over the front room walls while I was being spiritual with my stones.

The Moon Cloth

I've divided the cloth into three Moon cycles to fit in with the idea of the old Triple Goddess and the phases of the Maiden, Mother and Wise Woman.

I could have done it in four for the quarters of the Moon, or five, to include the actual New Moon and the Dark of the Moon; the last three days of the cycle when the Old Moon has vanished and we cannot yet see the New Moon although it is there. I've included the .New Moon in the first waxing circle, the innermost one; the Full Moon phase in the second circle and the Dark of the Moon as part of the *Waning* outer circle.

A woman's month, as well as her wider life span, seems to divide itself into thirds, rather than weeks or weeks plus bits, and what is important is what works, not what some man-made — or woman-made — ritual insists.

The inner Waxing circle

First draw your inner circle (drawing round a saucer will give you one about the right size, or you can do it freehand or use a compass). This *Waxing Circle* is marked with a third segment of moon left clear on the right and the rest filled in. Unlike the Sun, the Moon's movement is from right to left: so until Full Moon the light increases from the right. After Full Moon the dark increases from the right, giving you the full cycle.

This inner circle is the area of beginnings, whether short-term beginnings or major life

shifts. Stones that fall in this circle are rooted in
the initial enthusiasms and uncertainties and so
indicate that you may be feeling a bit vulnerable.

It's also a time for groundwork and the realisation that whatever you initiate will take time
and patience to bring to fruition. Also, since we
are talking about cycles and circles, it may be
that you have just come to the end of a particular phase in your life. And you could be feeling
a bit bruised and battered as you dust yourself
down, before picking yourself up and starting
all over again.

If a stone falls into this area upside down, with
its markings hidden, it can indicate that you are
not really sure that this new beginning is what
you want and are holding yourself back.

Now draw your middle circle (a tea plate is a
useful marker). This is the circle of the *Full
Moon* when full power is available and full

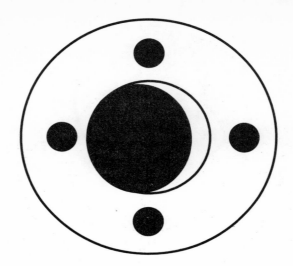

effort demanded. If you draw coloured moons
at 12, 3, 6 and 9 o'clock positions, this will
remind what the circle indicates (and looks
very mysterious!).

The Full Moon is a time for carrying out those
changes, asserting your demands and working
flat out because your energy is at its peak. And
so in relation to the stones, you can be confident that, whatever the issue, you've got the
wherewithal to carry it through and that you are
definitely on the right track.

So don't be fobbed off or persuaded to settle
for second best. If your stone is showing its
blank face you may feel as though you are
driving with your handbrake on. It may be
you're afraid of succeeding. If so, ask yourself
why.

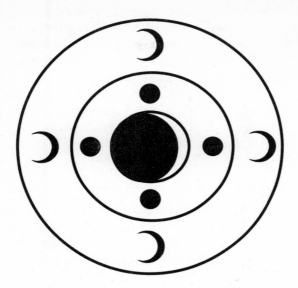

The third circle (dinner plate size) is that of the *Waning* or Dark of the Moon, which symbolises the time when you're running on the spot and definitely feel a couple of degrees under or a bit ratty.

So it's a good time for getting rid of the chaff and preparing the ground for those new beginnings. It's not a destructive time but one for recognising that there is a time and a season for every purpose under heaven. And it may be that this particular path is coming to an end.

If you throw a stone in this area, it's time to look at the obstacles and see whether the stone is telling you to move on. If the stone is hidden, it may suggest that the same mistakes keep

throwing a spanner in your works. Ask yourself why you need to keep replaying a particular scenario, whether it is little girl to someone
else's cross daddy, maiden to a self-styled fair
knight or victor to someone's victim.

As I said before, it is often what isn't said that
is the real agenda. Draw waning moons (with
a clear bit at the left) at 12 o'clock, 3 o'clock,
6 o'clock and 9.

Day 11

A cast of three

You don't need to remember all this before
moving on, it's summarised at the back. To
make it clearer we'll eavesdrop on someone
else's cast of three and in the next chapter you
can start using the circles.

Trina's reading

Trina is nineteen and, due to a job change, her
parents are moving from the town where she
has always lived to Wales. Trina says she is not
going with them and Nick, her current boyfriend, is pushing her to move in with him.

However, Trina has doubts about the perma-
nence of this relationship, though her parents'
opposition to Nick makes it hard for her to
admit it. At the moment Trina is unemployed,
but her father's firm has promised to help get
her on to an employment scheme in conjunction with a college in Wales.

Trina throws the **Sun**, which is hidden in her
outer circle of the *Waning Moon*. She then

throws **Earth** in her middle circle of the *Full
Moon* and power, and **Mars** in her *Waxing*
inner circle.

It might seem strange to find Trina's potential, represented by the Sun, in her Waning
Circle. At her age, all her abilities are waiting
to be realised.

But what it is really saying is that until Trina
recognises that a stage in her life is ending, she
will be stuck in her present role either as mum
and dad's little girl, or live-in-girlfriend in a
relationship she has doubts about.

So perhaps she should move to where she has
a work and training place on offer but with the

47

aim of getting her independence as soon as possible, perhaps even a live-in college place.

Earth in her *Full Moon* circle suggests that Trina can and should use her own resources and common sense to escape from the emotional issues and look at the nitty gritty of her future prospects. She should use her own abilities and energy, both of which are greater than she thinks, once she looks at the real issue of her own future and not her place in the scheme of other people's lives.

Mars in her *Waxing* circle shows that her resentment at being pushed about by other people is growing. If she's not careful, she could make a decision out of sheer defiance: i.e. move in with her boyfriend, not because she really wants to but simply because her parents forbid it.

Trina could channel her anger constructively to state in a determined way to all parties exactly what she wants. This may be to find a temporary job, to stay with other relations or friends for a while and to change her 'new phase' from resentment into positive steps to find what she really wants for herself.

The present economic climate does make it difficult for young people to be independent. But Trina knows in her heart that her boyfriend isn't really offering her freedom but just a different form of the control that her parents have over her.

What if your stone should fall outside the circles? In our Moon Magic, the area outside the circles, and indeed, anywhere on the floor or table where your stone may land is the Solar region. I've based this on the old Celtic Wheel of Time, but concentrated the main Moon Cloth on the Solar festivals, the Solstices and Equinoxes because these are times of the year we still recognise today.

Day 12

The outer part of the Moon Cloth

In the Celtic year there were eight major landmarks and two seasons winter and summer. The Moon played an important role and the interspersed Moon and Fire festivals were linked to pastoral and agricultural events. Months began at Full Moon and days were measured from Sunset to Sunset. The dates were very fluid as the whole system was based on lunar calculations.

So that's why our Moon Cloth begins on December 21, which marks the Mid-Winter Solstice or shortest Day. In the Celtic system the New Year began at the beginning of November on the fire festival of Samhain. For simplicity, we will begin by using only the four solar landmarks for the outside area of the Moon Cloth. Later in the book I will describe a slightly more complicated version.

We'll begin our *Winter* three-month segment at 12 o'clock in the north, the Winter Solstice and shortest day and longest night. This time of year was recognised by earliest civilisations as a time when it was feared the sun was dying. So bonfires were lit and evergreen boughs were used to persuade the sun to rise again and the crops to grow. Our Christmas festivities today have their roots in this early magical practice.

Draw a dark Sun because this is a solar division and a straight line from the outer edge of the cloth to the outermost circle.

Winter

The point at which we'll begin our *Spring* segment is at 3 o'clock, the East, the Spring Equinox when day and night are equal. The Spring or Vernal Equinox, often associated with Easter was the time when hens began to lay again and these first eggs were given as tribute to the goddess Eostre.

Draw a Sun rising in the east (plain side to the left) and a straight line from the edge of the cloth to the outermost circle.

Our *Summer* segment begins at 6 o'clock. The Summer Solstice, the longest day and shortest night, was a time when flaming sun wheels were raced down hills to celebrate the triumph of Baldur, the sun god.

Draw an uncoloured Sun and a straight line from the edge of the cloth to the outermost circle.

Summer

The *Autumn* segment begins at 9 o'clock, the Autumn Equinox, when day and night are equal once more. This was traditionally the time of the second harvest, a time when harvest festivals and suppers are held in urban as well as rural churches.

Draw a Sun setting in the West (its plain side is still in the east but, because of its position on the cloth, the dark side will now be facing towards the centre of the cloth). Then draw a straight line from the edge of the cloth to the outermost circle.

Spring

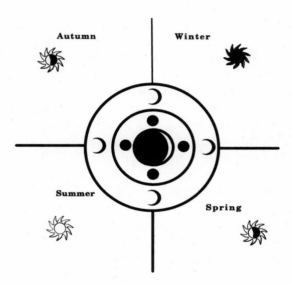

Each segment begins at a solstice or equinox, because that is a good way of getting in touch with the Solar clock which runs clock-wise (unlike the Moon which, of course, turns moonwise or anti-clockwise) and marks the seasons of our year and our life.

The Solstice   These seasons may be a time to wait and trust at the winter solstice, a time to make new plans at the vernal equinox, a time for full power at the summer solstice and a time for contemplation, looking back as well as forward at the autumn equinox.

Women need to refer to a solar clock to regulate their life in the outer world, the world dominated by machines and men.

When a stone falls in one of these four outer solar segments, you will know that the pull of the outer world and external circumstances are very strong and that the time scale of events is slower than for the inner circles. Beginnings at the spring equinox may not be fulfilled till the autumn.

The true solar calendar isn't linear. We have just made life that way. It runs in a never-ending cycle.

One season follows another and each must be lived through, enjoyed for what they are and then left behind if we are to lead a balanced existence. Dreading a coming season or mourning one that has just passed, are two equally destructive ways of living.

So if your stones fall in a solar area, they will probably be talking to you about your need to react in a positive and creative way to the changes imposed by others, or by what is sometimes called fate.

You may prefer to call your solar segments by the seasonal names but some women find it helpful to think of them as special times that convey the meaning in the name.

On my cloth, stones that fall into the outer segment between March 21 and June 21 are in the **Spring** segment. Spring is sometimes called *The Time of Sowing* and whether the calendar on the wall says January or June, when your stone falls here you may find yourself propelled into a new situation not necessarily of your choosing.

Or it may be that a new relationship could develop, or even a phase in a relationship that wasn't what you had planned or hoped for.

For, as we've said, these solar segments mark out the external influences beyond your control, though of course we all influence 'fate' by our own actions or lack of action. Many a bailiff out of the blue began with a pile of unopened brown envelopes.

When you're hit by this new factor, whether or not you contributed to it, on the whole it will be easier to take the step before you, rather than paddling your canoe furiously against the tide or hiding under the blankets.

If your stone is hidden in the *Time of Sowing*, then you may be clinging on to what you know in your heart is no longer secure or viable and closing your ears and eyes to the inevitable.

The Time of Nurturing The outer segment between June 21 and September 21 is the **Summer** segment. Summer, or the *Time of Nurturing*, represents a period when you will be called upon to do a lot of hard graft. The lazy days of summer are over.

Accept that, at this phase in your life, you may be forced to take on responsibilities and opportunities that you feel you aren't capable of dealing with. You may also have to put in a great deal of effort for no immediate benefit.

The old biblical maxim 'As ye sow so shall ye reap', left out this vital stage of keeping up the impetus while the seeds are growing. Time and nature won't do it all, whether it's a busy-Lizzy plant or a relationship that you happen to be cultivating.

Nice though it would be if we could sit back and depend upon magic, nothing will happen without a lot of slog and sleepless nights on your part.

If your stone is hidden in the *Time of Nurturing*, then you may be putting obstacles in your own path or still paddling around in the shallows, waiting for the right moment to put that great new plan into operation.

What is holding you back, inertia or a fear of failure? It might be that you are listening to yesterday's record, one that should be dumped in the attic once and for all.

Autumn, or the *Time of Gathering*, is the segment between September 21 and December 21. This area involves looking backwards as well as forwards, of assessing your successes and planning your next move.

As you become more aware of these natural seasons, whether you live in the city or country, you may find that your life does pass through seasonal highs and lows. It's known that lack of sunshine causes depression. But if you can go with the natural order then life does flow more harmoniously, whether you live by the solar or lunar clock or a mixture of the two.

If your stone is hidden in the *Time of Gathering*, you may be hoping that someone else will make the decisions for you, or come up with the ideal solution to the 'Where next?' question. What are you looking for? A permanent overdraft at nil per cent interest, a cruise on the QE2? Unfortunately, no one's picking up the tab except you, unless you are prepared to pay a very high price tomorrow for an easy ride today.

Winter, or the *Time of Waiting* takes us to the top of our clock and we can only hope and trust, whichever gods or goddesses we try to placate, that spring will follow this dismal time of the year for the season and the soul.

But dismal or not, winter is a vital season. We may not be able to huddle in our hut and hope the supplies last out. There is always work to be

The Time of Waiting

done, even when snow is on the ground. But this is a time in our lives for withdrawing into ourselves.

For when it becomes clear that we aren't going anywhere fast, at least we have the time to come to terms with the fact that, however much we love and are loved, we are separate and we can't rewrite history whether we are seventeen or seventy.

And so, in a way, it is a rich time to concentrate on what is important to us deep down.

If you get a stone in the **Winter** or *Time of Waiting* segment, then it is probably time to withdraw for a while from the frantic activity of everyday life and to take time to get in touch with your unconscious side.

It is a time to listen to your dreams and to slow right down so that you have time just to relax and rejoice in your unique qualities.

If your stone is hidden in the *Time of Waiting*, then perhaps you are confusing loneliness and being alone. You can be lonely no matter how many people you are with.

Perhaps you have found that out lately and your present lifestyle may actually be keeping you in a situation where you feel isolated inside. Sometimes you have to be alone for a time before you can find happiness in the company of others.

Now you can do your first cast of three. Put all the stones you have marked into the bag, draw one out at a time without looking and throw it in the rough direction of the cloth.

1. **What is the stone?**
2. **Is it hidden?**
3. **In which area does it land?**

A cast of three

Do the same for all three stones. You may prefer to throw the stones and then look at them. If they are close together, they will be related. But if they fly off in all directions them maybe you are feeling a bit fragmented.

Sometimes a stone will knock another out of position or land on top of another. It may well reflect the way you feel that life is knocking you about at the moment.

Now let's eavesdrop on a reading where all three stones fell in the outer segments.

Anne's reading
Anne is married with three young children and is in her late thirties. She is due to go to Open University Summer School and her husband had agreed to take care of the children.

But his friends at work have been telling him that this is just an excuse for her to have a good time and now he is starting to raise objections and to make snide remarks. Is it worthwhile going or should she cancel her week away? Anne asks.

A reading for Anne

Anne throws the **Sun** hidden in the *Time of Gathering* (Autumn), the **Moon** hidden in the Time of Nurturing (Summer) and **Mercury** in the *Time of Sowing* (Spring).

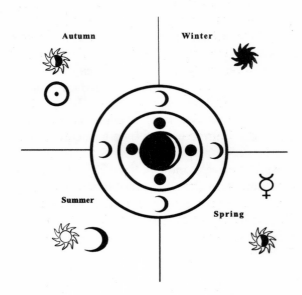

Many a New Man falters before the traditional chauvinism of his mates. The **Sun** clearly represents the way that Anne's efforts to fulfil her potential have hit the first major hurdle.

If Anne lets her husband sway her decisions, then she is only going to store up trouble in future. For if she doesn't go, then she may well end up feeling frustrated and bitter and trying to push her children along the path that she failed to take herself.

The **Moon** tells Anne to listen to her own judgments not those of others and again warns her against taking the line of least resistance.

The fact that the **Moon** is hidden in Summer, the *Time of Nurturing*, suggests that she may, unconsciously, be going along with her husband's insinuations that it's not right that she should go off and enjoy herself, even though she will be working on the course.

But she must remember — and make it clear to him — that life on the campus is not going to be all Lambrusco and discos. Not if she really wants her qualifications, which she does.

Mercury in the *Time of Sowing* (Spring), marks a clear need for communication at the beginning of a new stage in her relationship with her husband i.e. her first bid for independence.

They may need to talk over the real issues, not the half-truths, and perhaps she could compromise. Perhaps they could rent a flat on the campus for the family so her husband can see she is attending a university not a non-stop orgy.

This might seem like Anne is giving way to male chauvinism and, in an ideal world, she would say 'Blow you' and go on to fulfil her destiny.

But we know that in the real world life is

seldom like that, especially where children are involved. Women have to make all sorts of efforts and compromises to inch their way to a better life. By taking this option, at least Anne will be able to do what she wants, and keep her family, rather than being forced to choose between them.

Even if there is no crisis like this looming in your life, you can still do your daily stone reading, using it to home in on the prevalent issue of the day. You may find that, even as you make more stones to choose from, certain stones appear time and time again.

A full reading using the circles may be useful once or twice a week or whenever you have an important decision to make.

If you can, then you should try to do it when you won't be disturbed. I sometimes have to wait till after eleven at night when the last of my little insomniacs has finally collapsed.

Presuming that you can get a little bit of personal time and space, then why not make it a special occasion.

Light candles if you feel like it, to get that soft lighting effect, put on your favourite mood music and make yourself a warm drink. If you can, turn the time you make for your reading into a very special 'you' time. Then, even if the news from the Stones is not good, things won't be all bad.

Jupiter was king of the Roman Gods and, like his Greek counterpart Zeus, he had thunderbolts for weapons, carried by his eagle. **Jupiter** became associated with justice, honour and power, a sort of super-Roman Emperor: stiff upper lip in a crisis, smiling benignly as he dispensed wisdom and justice, and not above a virginal frown when the rules are broken or a giggle uttered in the wrong place.

In the solar system, **Jupiter** is the largest planet, taking nearly twelve years to orbit the Sun and is largely made up of gases. His sign is simply a half circle joined to a cross, the spiritual potential for life joined to the cross of matter (the elements).

2

Jupiter

For us, the Planet Stone **Jupiter** represents the conventional path to success and fulfilment, the work ethic and material achievement — not by dirty dealing but by logically stepping from A to B to C, as befits the King of the Sky Gods.

This stone deals with justice and with making your pathway to the stars using the map, taking the exams or saving the deposit for your new flat.

Jupiter is not naturally a woman's stone and certainly not one that I feel a great affinity for. But, unfortunately, that's to my cost because I'm a great corner-cutter and very often I end up trying to explain my mistakes to a Jove-type figure, who isn't at all amused.

Jupiter

If you get **Jupiter** in a reading, then the chances are that this time you are not going to get in by the back door, or by one of those inspirational leaps that can get women out of trouble. Instead, you can get on only by following the conventional path.

There's no point in hoping to cut corners or get away with a sneaky flyer. The report has got to be written and be perfectly presented, the forms have got to be filled in and you've got to wait for the wheels to grind into motion.

You may not be very pleased when **Jupiter** turns up, because he usually arrives at a stage when you want to dot someone on the nose because they've wronged someone you love.

But there are official channels and now is the time to use them. I've got to finish writing about **Jupiter**, even though he annoys me, because the system needs his balance and all feeling, all intuition and no solid basis won't get me far right now. So stop and listen to Jupiter and, for once, do it by the book.

When **Jupiter** is hidden, it may be indicating that you have been taking one chance too many because you've been lucky in the past. Open those brown envelopes right now. Study for your exam.

Accept that you may not like the guy running the system, but he pays your wages, so save the James Dean bit for the movies.

Saturn, the ringed planet and another giant, is even further out in space than Jupiter and takes 29 and a half years to orbit the Sun. Its density is less than that of water and, like Jupiter, it is largely gaseous, with possibly a solid or metallic hydrogen core.

Its sign is **Jupiter** in reverse, with the cross followed by the half circle at the bottom, suggesting the potential is weighed down in limitation and death.

Saturn

In mythology, **Saturn** was Jupiter's father who was driven from the sky by his son. **Saturn** wasn't top of the paternal popularity stakes due to an unfortunate habit of devouring his children. He is associated with the Greek god Cronus (Father Time) and was sent off to Italy where, as the agricultural god, he reigned in the legendary Golden Age which was remembered in the annual knees-up of Saturnalia when anything went.

Saturn is very much the shadow side of **Jupiter** and in our system represents all those old burdens we carry around weighing us down: the old guilts, the negative bits we pretend don't belong to us and all our failures from Brownies onwards.

Above all, he shows us the suitcase of 'if onlys' we carry (If I'd married my first love, back packed round the world instead of getting a job in the bank, gone to college instead of getting married and having kids, got divorced,

The Solstice not got remarried, been two inches taller, blonde-haired and three stone lighter).

The 'if only' bag is the heaviest of all the burdens that we carry in our heads. Every time we stop to dip in to it and brood over all our unfulfilled dreams, we simply slow ourselves down in the real world.

When **Saturn** appears in a reading it probably indicates that you are letting the past dominate the present and that old resentments and regrets may be preventing you from making the most of the benefits of here and now. The first love, the missed opportunity, should be relegated to **Saturn's** mythical Golden Age, that perhaps was not quite so wonderful, if we take off our rose-tinted spectacles and view it in the cold light of day.

So shed your self-imposed limitations that may be holding you back as much as the buffetings of life and go from where you are now with the resources you have at your disposal.

When **Saturn** is hidden you may be playing that old guilt harp yourself and loading on to others your own lack of achievement or happiness which may not be down to them.

Make sure that you are blaming them fairly for their own sins and omissions and not for the unresolved wrongs of your mum, dad or past partner.

Uranus is one of the three 'modern' planets and the first to be discovered by telescope in 1781 by William Herschel. It is a huge planet and so far from the Sun it takes 84 years to complete its orbit. , **Uranus** the god was the son of Gaea, the Earth.

In Greek mythology she bore him, 'the sky crowned with stars'. He and Gaea bore twelve Titans, one of whom was Cronus (we met him as Saturn) and various monsters including the Cyclopes.

Uranus shut his children in the Earth but Cronus, aided by his mother, overthrew **Uranus**. This involved a particularly nasty mutilation with a sickle, best not imagined at tea-time. The planets have some nasty skeletons in their cupboards.

Uranus

To draw **Uranus** simply put a TV aerial on top of a circle.

Uranus represents the need for a new approach to an old problem that is bugging you, or to a sudden disruption to your daily life that may at first seem unwelcome.

I don't advocate the Cronus solution, though the anger of **Mars** is sometimes useful in getting change underway.

Whatever your problem, rather than choosing between the pit of snakes or the cage of tigers it may be necessary to seek out a different route, maybe using the inspiration of the **Moon**. It's surprising how often in a woman's reading of three stones **Uranus** appears with **Mars** and the **Moon**. You will find as you use the system that the stone meanings do fit together.

If you get **Uranus**, then it is more than likely that the old tried and tested answers that you usually trot out to deal with the problems of life, don't fit the new situation or problem and an original approach is needed.

Though this may not be a change you sought it is a way out of stagnation. Much creative thinking and many life changes have been carried out under the auspices of **Uranus**.

So the question facing you is not 'Should I?' but 'How?'. The idea of taking an entirely original approach may seem terrifying at first, but you may surprise yourself (and everybody else) when you try it. And in six months time it is more likely than not that you will be very glad you made the change, whether it was in the personal or work sphere.

When **Uranus** is hidden, then you are probably looking at the negative side of the change. But your fears are using up valuable energy at a time when it should be all systems go.

So concentrate on the logistics for whatever enterprise you have in hand and worry about the metaphysics when you've made that necessary leap into the unknown.

Sometimes it is useful to look at daily readings over a longer period to see whether the same stones keep appearing.

Hilary's reading

Hilary is a business woman in her fifties. Her firm has been computerised and she feels at a disadvantage to her younger colleagues who have taken like ducks to water to the new system. The pile of manuals remain untouched on Hilary's desk and she has made excuses for not going on the training courses which have been offered.She argues that the system is dehumanising the business and that the old ways are the best.

A Planet
Stones
reading
over six
days

Her immediate junior has accused her of being afraid of failing, something which Hilary vigorously denies. But she now feels that she is being undermined.From a full set of the planet stones, Hilary draws:

Day 1. **Uranus**   ♅

Day 2. **Uranus**   ♅

Day 3. **Jupiter**   ♃

Day 4. **Saturn**   ♄

Day 5. **Uranus**   ♅

Day 6. **Jupiter**   ♃

Two **Jupiter** and three **Uranus** stones. Hilary's inner powers are certainly trying to tell her something.

The strong showing by **Uranus** highlights what seems to be disruptive change to the safe world that Hilary knew. But the change need not be destructive, even though she is obviously very worried by it.

It could even be a step forward for her if, by adapting her way of thinking to a new mode, she can actually use the computer system to ease the routine aspects of her work. She could then give herself more time for the human aspect of the job which is obviously so important to her.

So the real question which is facing her is not 'Should I go for it?'. If she wants to keep her position, she has to go with the flow and change her ways, however painful this is. It is just a waste of energy to go on arguing the rights and wrongs of the situation.

The real question that she must answer is 'How do I go for it?'. And that leads to the two **Jupiters**, which are pushing her into taking the conventional approach. This is that she must work slowly and surely from A to Z without relying on the intuitive leaps which have helped her so much in the past.

There isn't any alternative to reading those manuals, going on the training course and, if necessary, asking for extra time and help to master what is an unfamiliar way of operating.

Computer literacy doesn't need any special abilities but it does have to be learned, however much it may go against the grain. Hilary admitted that she had faced other difficult challenges before and had been able to settle down and master them.

The next question is: what is the real reason for her resistance to change this time round?

The appearance of **Saturn**, which can have a very negative aspect, gives us a clue. It is very likely that her junior did strike a raw nerve with that casual remark about Hilary's fear of failing.

Fear of failure is something we all have to live with — especially when we have done well at something because then there is so much further to fall.

But it is no good hiding behind the way things were. That can only hold us back from embracing change when change has to come and making the best of it.

Hidden deep in Hilary's mental luggage may be a lot of old put-downs from way back. Perhaps at school she was told that she was useless at maths or no good at learning new things. These little hurts should have been left behind in the classroom when she left school

A reading for Hilary

and entered the real world where she *has* made a success of her life, no matter what some snide schoolmarm might have said to her when she was still in a gym slip.

Even when we are old and grey, it is difficult to ignore the negative voice of **Saturn** which wails at us down the years — echoing the disapproving tones of a teacher, parent, elder brother or sister, or disapproving 'friend'.

But the stones are telling Hilary that if she can learn to look forward and not backward, she can succeed — as long as she enters the new field with enthusiasm and is prepared to learn a new skill.

A reading for yourself

Having seen how the stones worked for Hilary, you might like to look back at your readings for the last six days to see if any pattern is emerging, even though you have not learned all the stones yet.

Don't forget to use your circles and to use the definitions at the back as often as you like. If you feel that it would be helpful, re-read the chapters and, if it's all getting a bit too much, feel free to take a few days off before going on.

There is no need to rush.

After all, we are working in Moon Time.

Neptune is another recent discovery in planetary terms. It was first sighted in 1846 though its existence was predicted three years earlier by the Cambridge mathematician John Couch Adams and the French astronomer Le Verrier. It is much further away than Uranus and takes 165 years to orbit the Sun. On the mythological front, after **Saturn** was dethroned, **Jupiter** gave his brother **Neptune** (Poseidon to the Greeks) the sea as his dominion.

His symbol of power was the trident or three-pronged spear which he used to shatter rocks, summon up or banish storms and shake the shores.

Neptune

His symbol is very easy to remember. Draw his trident with a cross attached to it at the bottom on your planet stone.

In our Moon magic, **Neptune**, being the watery planet, is linked with emotions and sensitivity.

At its best, it represents our ability to see beneath the surface issues and to be receptive to the moods and feelings of others. A fluid, empathic approach to people and life can avoid many unnecessary conflicts and enable us to adapt to the needs of the situation.

On the other hand, it's important not to let sentiment cloud your judgment or to don rose-coloured spectacles. Your gut feeling is the best guide as to whether a person or situation is rock solid. So if you feel you are being conned, then don't allow your desire for a happy ending override what you know deep down.

If you get **Neptune** in a reading, the surface situation is not what it seems. Tune in to what people mean and feel and not to what they say or do. You will probably need to be highly adaptable if other people's feelings are running high and they've painted themselves into a corner. So it's a time for tact and gentle persuasion rather than brute force (however tempting that is).

When **Neptune** is hidden, you may be dreaming of bunnies, red hearts and roses. But the essential thing is not to get so carried away, either by sentiment, or by the illusion that the job is done and you can put your feet up for the easy ride all the way home.

You can spend so long dreaming of the handsome prince who will whisk you away to exotic isles, that you may miss out on the perfectly acceptable guy in the office who offers you a day trip to Bognor.

If you are the type who prefers to risk having nothing, rather than compromising your own dreams, then that is fine. But be sure that you are making this choice consciously and with your eyes open. **Neptune** is telling you that this is definitely a time to listen to your gut feeling, while going through the small print of any offers with a strong magnifying glass.

Pluto was not tracked down until 1930 by Clyde Tombaugh though its existence was predicted in 1914. It takes 248 years to revolve around the Sun and is a small frozen body covered with frozen gases. Its orbit is so strange that for part of its journey round the Sun it is closer in than Neptune.

In classical mythology, **Pluto** (Dis to the Greeks) was the god of the Underworld. He was given this kingdom after the overthrow of his father, **Saturn**, and was perhaps best remembered for carrying off Proserpine into his realms to have his evil way.

Pluto

Pluto is very easy to draw. It is like a rearranged Mercury symbol with the circle on top and an upturned half circle not touching underneath, with a cross joining the half-circle at the bottom.

In our Moon Magic, **Pluto** is the symbol for letting go what is no longer needed in our lives, whether it's a redundant stage in your life or a relationship that's run its course, or even an interest that once excited us but is now a chore.

We are all creatures of habit and don't always recognise when the party's over and it is time to leave. This holds true either in the case of the child who is facing up to the fact that she is of an age to leave home, or the older woman who must accept the end of her childbearing years. It is a time to accept we should let younger people take over our jobs or, if the kids have

The Solstice flown the nest, to accept that we shouldn't still relate to our partners purely in terms of being parents.

But **Pluto** does not only relate to the older woman. Even young women have to learn to let go. After the first love affair we have to leave our childhood and accept that there aren't blacks and whites but usually dingy grey.

It's not all doom and gloom, however. Because once we've cleared out that old attic and opened the windows to admit change in our life, then we can go out and make all those dreams that can still be fulfilled and release the energies used in trying to hold on to what cannot be any more.

So **Pluto** isn't just about endings but beginnings too and that can make it a very positive stone to throw.

If you get **Pluto** in a reading then you may be at a natural change point or looking at your safe familiar world with jaundiced eyes. It's never easy to close a door. This is particularly true as we get older and a bit life-shocked, because, if we are not careful, we can cling on to some pretty unlovable devils simply because they are familiar, rather than step into the unknown.

But we can't open new doors till we've said goodbye to a particular stage, relationship or situation that is redundant and making us feel tired or restless and not looking forward to the new day. So be brave and set your sights on the next part of the journey.

When **Pluto** is hidden, it may be we are planning a backward step to stop us confronting the real issue. If your last baby has started school, is pregnancy really the answer to the emptiness you feel in your life or marriage? Are you entering into a new relationship a bit too quickly because you fear being alone? Whatever the backward step, ask yourself why you are taking it and be sure it is really what you want.

Day 21

For the really big issues or about once a week for an overview, it's a good idea to use six stones in a reading. This is simply throwing two lots of three. But with more stones you can see from the positions on the cloth what is happening inside you.

A reading with six Planet Stones

For instance, the six stones may scatter to the four winds and you may realise that this sums up exactly how you feel: just as if everything is going in different directions at once and, try as you might, you can't get it together.

On the other hand, the stones might all end up lying in a heap or one on top of the other. This suggests that all the different aspects are linked and are affecting your life as a whole.

If a stone knocks another out of the way, ten to one something important in your life has been sent flying. Once you see the positions, it's easier to work out how to fit the bits of your life together.

Generally, the cloth is like a mirror to your unconscious and if things are hunky-dory in one area then it won't appear as an issue. What do turn up are those psychic spots and blemishes that you can either try to get rid of or accept.

Either way, you are making the decisions for yourself and not letting other people either consciously or unconsciously manipulate your destiny.

To demonstrate we shall eavesdrop once again on someone else's reading.

Sally's Reading

Sally is in her early thirties and does not have anyone special in her life. Since her husband left her for another woman five years ago, every relationship she tries to form ends abruptly when she asks for a commitment from her new potential partner.

There has been no shortage of boyfriends but the affairs tend to be passionate and instant. Then they fizzle out once Sally makes it clear that she's looking for more than fleeting excitement.

Sally wants to know what she is doing wrong because time is running out if she is to have the family that she craves So she takes a full set of the Planet Stones and throws:

Stone 1. **Pluto** in her inner circle of the *Waxing Moon*

Stone 2. **Mars** hidden in her Solar *Time of Winter or Waiting*.

Stone 3. **Neptune** in the middle circle of the *Full Moon*.

Stone 4. **Uranus** in the inner circle in the *Waxing Moon*.

Stone 5. **Mercury** hidden in the inner circle of the *Waxing Moon*.

Stone 6. **Venus** hidden in the middle circle of the *Full Moon*.

There's a lot happening in the circle of the *Waxing Moon*. Three out of the six stones fall here. So we need to look at Sally's new beginnings and why they never seem to get beyond the initial stage.

Pluto, the first stone, seems an odd one to find here for it talks about letting a redundant stage go.

But what it is suggesting is that until Sally lets go of her overriding need for a permanent relationship leading to a child above all other considerations, her dealings with other people

A reading for Sally

Mars hidden in the
Time of Winter

Pluto
Uranus
Mercury
(hidden)
all in the
inner circle
of the
Waxing Moon

Neptune
Venus
(hidden)
in the
circle
of the
Full Moon

will not be able to develop naturally. Men do get very worried if they feel they are valued only for the function they will serve in a woman's master plan. It's not surprising they do a runner when the pressure is on.

If men are seen only as potential life partners, this will stand in the way of meaningful inter-actions that are the first step to any permanent relationship, whether friendship or love.

Mars is hidden in the Solar area of *Winter* or the *Time of Waiting,* indicating that Sally may be confusing loneliness with being alone. **Mars** suggests she still feels a great deal of anger over her marriage. Perhaps she does need a period without heavy emotional involvement to heal the wounds and to learn to love herself as an individual and not only define her success as being part of a twosome.

The solar aspect of the stone (emphasised because it fell outside the circle) suggests that this healing may require a longer time scale than she had planned. But she is still relatively young. When the biological clock is ticking away, this can override all other considera-tions. Even dedicated career women take sneaky trips round Mothercare. But Sally has to sort out her own conflicts before she can even start to think about family ties.

Neptune in the middle circle of the *Full Moon* hints that it is important for Sally to be aware of the underlying mood of future en-

counters and not make the other person feel
pressurised into commitment before he is ready.

If she becomes sensitive to the deeper emotions in any relationship, then she will instinctively know when to hold back and when to
reveal her feelings. It is only her feeling of
anxiety that she is a failure in love that blocks
this natural ability.

Uranus is in the inner circle of the *Waxing
Moon* and so to rebuild her life Sally needs a
new approach to her dilemma.

Rather than asking herself what might be
wrong with her, perhaps she should try to
concentrate on making herself a social life and
a new circle of friends.

When having a relationship simply for the
sake of having a relationship stops being the
be-all and end-all of her life, she may well find
that it happens naturally.

Mercury hidden (blank face uppermost) in
the circle of the *Waxing Moon* says that most of
the real communication is going on in Sally's
head and that she doesn't share her fears and
feelings with prospective partners. This might
make them more understanding of her insecu-
rity.

If she could explain her lack of trust, then she
could gain reassurance that she won't be be-
trayed, which is what she really is seeking,

though she appears to be asking for permanent commitment.

Venus hidden in the circle of the *Full Moon* shows that the stumbling block to attaining a permanent relationship, is that Sally is looking at every new male as a potential life partner and not as a person with faults and virtues.

If she can look at each person as he is she will not be disillusioned if he does have feet of clay. Sally may even decide that she doesn't want him as a life partner when she looks at the actual person, warts and all. The reading of six offers no magic answers plucked from the sky, no handsome princes or guarantees of happy ever after.

Whatever the traditional fortune tellers say, no one can guarantee that fairy-tale ending. If you believe a load of false promises about tomorrow, the danger is that you won't make the most of today. But Sally, like all who use the Planet Stones or any other system of personal divination, can find happiness if she doesn't waste time agonising over what she hasn't got, but makes the best of what she has.

If she meets the man of her dreams, then it's a bonus. But it is not necessary for a very fulfilled life. Being alone isn't the same as being lonely and only when we can face and love ourselves can we really find happiness with, if not through, others.

A reading for yourself

Now try your own reading of six and don't forget to note it in your Moon diary. Find a time when you won't be disturbed and try to make your Moon divination time happy and relaxed in the way you like best. You might find it useful to note any dreams you have following your reading as there may be all kinds of clues as to the best course to take.

Your daily stone should be building up a representative picture of what is going on in your world and you may find the same stones do keep appearing. See what your psychic Jiminy Cricket is saying.

Day 22

The Blank Stone

There is now only one planet stone to learn, that is the undiscovered planet, that astronomers believe is just there waiting to be identified, somewhere on the outskirts of the solar system, beyond Pluto. So for now just leave this planet stone blank. But who knows? In our lifetime we may yet learn its name.

It represents our destiny, our future which we have not yet made because we haven't travelled possible paths and, more importantly, reached the crossroads where only we can ultimately choose the route.

We tend to be afraid of blanks in our life, empty days in a diary especially at weekends. We shut the curtains after dark and watch television or play music rather than face the silence and our inner thoughts. We stimulate our children from birth, even before, and rush them from activity to activity.

And yet, if we are just quiet, not doing anything but just being, we can discover a whole new dimension for ourselves alone — the quiet inner core where the inner voice and our unconscious wisdom reside.

So the **Blank** stone is to be welcomed in our readings and in our life. This stone may well turn up at a crunch time when there is no clearcut answer and conventional wisdom fails. That, too, is to be welcomed for we can leave the old restrictions behind along with the messages of yesterday. Freed from the luggage we no longer need, we can move forward.

The **Blank** stone corresponds to the Stone of Fate, the Wyrd Stone in the Runic system and to the Fool in the Tarot system.

And like the Fool who isn't foolish at all, it's a stone of intuition and inspiration and all those functions we have and yet so often leave undeveloped.

The **Blank** Stone does not mean that you are left on your own and friendless with no direction home. Instead it urges you to use your basic instincts. It combines all the best qualities of the other Planet Stones and all that is best within you.

It represents amalgamation of experience

and untapped potential which you possess as a
unique individual.

You may be alone but you are not helpless.
You are guided by your inner star. It's the key
to inner magic whether this system or any other
and it's worth spending time on.

Think of the real change points in your life
when you went for broke.

Even if you fell flat on your face now and
then, at least you had the glorious feeling of
being in charge of your life.

How grey the 'if-onlys' seem in comparison,
the trip we never took, the time we took a
chance and enjoyed pure happiness and excitement.

I remember at school being read a poem by
T.S. Eliot in which he talked about these times
as *'sudden in a shaft of sunlight'* and said
*'ridiculous the waste sad time stretching be-
fore and after'*.

Like many teenagers with all my life before
me, I was more interested in boys, records and
clothes.

But now, with more than my share of 'if
onlys', I know that we have got to grab those
golden moments while we can and sometimes
throw caution to the winds.

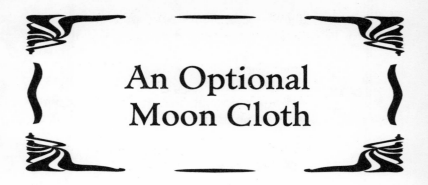

An Optional
Moon Cloth

Your Moon Cloth will give you accurate readings on any issue and at any level. But because the Celtic fire festivals are linked with the Moon, I'll suggest an alternative cloth which you might like to draw on the back of your moon cloth. Use it when you are thinking of an inner issue or something beyond the everyday world.

You could be really clever and combine the two cloths so that you have eight outer segment markings. But there is no need for that unless you feel it would be really helpful to you.

Read this section even if you're sticking to the first cloth as it may give you some background to the ideas that have fascinated me and that seem very relevant to women's lives today.

The first three circles are exactly the same: the inner circle is the *Waxing Moon,* containing all those new beginnings and plans you're ready

Day
23

An optional
Moon Cloth

An optional Moon Cloth to initiate; the *Full Moon* represents you at the height of your power and the *Waning Moon* deals with endings and a withdrawal into your inner world.

The first segment, *Winter,* begins at the north-west compass position and is dated at the evening of November 2, remembering that Celtic festivals went on over three days.

The Celtic winter began at Samhain on October 31, equivalent to the Christian All-Souls Eve that is still celebrated as Hallowe'en. During the three-day festival, the cattle were brought in or slaughtered for the winter needs and it was a rest time as our Christmas is supposed to be today. Herdsmen came down from the hills for the winter and food was left out for family ghosts who were believed to come in shivering from the fields. Draw your first winter line, about halfway between 10 and 11 on a clock face, as a diagonal line.

Day

24

Spring

The second segment, *Spring,* begins in the north-east compass position. On the eve of January 31 there began another three-day lunar fire festival, Oimelc or Brigantia, when the first lambs were born and fresh ewes' milk was available to the community after the worst of the winter. It was a time sacred to the maiden aspect of the Goddess and has survived today in the Outer Hebrides as the festival of Brigit (who merged with the Christian St Bride).

This is marked between 1 o'clock and 2 as a diagonal line.

Day 25

Summer

The third segment, *Summer,* begins in the south-east compass position. The Celtic Summer began on Beltane, the eve of April 30, when the cattle were let out of barns and purified of disease by driving them between two fires. Belenos or Baldur was the solar god.

This is the origin of our May Day revels and many of the ancient rituals practised today, such as Maypole dancing, have their origins in this early fertility festival. Draw this line diagonally between 4 and 5 on a traditional clock face.

The fourth segment, *Autumn,* begins in the south-west compass position. Lughnasadh (pronounced loon-assa) or Lammas, July 31, marked High Summer, the Feast of The Goddess of the Land when the first hay was harvested and as an added bonus you could try out a new partner for a year and a day! Draw this line diagonally between 7 and 8 on a traditional clock face.

These fire festival divisions have exactly the same meanings as the solar ones. *Winter* still means a time of trust and waiting, *Spring* a time of making new plans and starting new ventures, *Summer* the golden days of your power and nurturing efforts and Autumn a time to reap, gather in, assess and start to slow down.

**An optional
Moon Cloth**

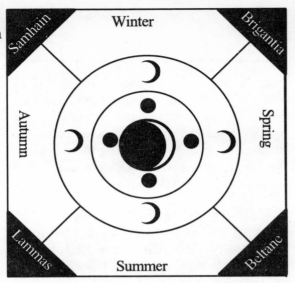

When a stone is hidden, again, it is a time to see what's happening below the surface and what, or who, is holding you back.

You may find you are making obstacles for yourself without realising it. Ask yourself why and if you really want change right now. If, in your heart of hearts, you find that you don't, then accept that you, and only you, are in control and go with your inner flow, whatever the outside world is screaming or demanding.

But you will probably find that the meanings apply to your inner spiritual world, rather than to actual events or your daily life and relationships. You may wish to use this cloth for yourself alone.

A Fire Cloth Reading

You may like to use your new Cloth with Fire Festival divisions instead of your *Solar Outer Segment* divisions at different times according to your mood. I have the two cloths on opposite sides of a scarf and use the *solar divisions* if it's an outer, worldly matter and the lunar fire festival segments for an inner, personal issue. But, as I have said, the alternative cloth is purely optional and you may want to stick with either one of the other version.

Terri's Reading

Terri, who is in her late forties, has separated from her husband. She has not seen her teenage daughter, Sophie, for several months, since she left her husband to live with a man with a young family. Sophie hates the family for whom her mum left home and refused to go with her mother, or even visit the flat she rents with her new partner.

This led to stilted meetings in cafes that have now dried up and Sophie won't answer Terri's letters or phone calls. Though it seemed an external worldly issue, Terri wanted to use the Moon Cloth with the fire festival divisions.

Terri cast **Pluto** hidden in the outer area of *Winter* (between Hallowe'en, the Celtic New Year and Brigantia at the beginning of February when the ewes gave their first milk and the first shoots appeared).

Her second stone, **Mars,** fell in the outer area of *Spring* between Brigantia and Beltane (on April 30, the beginning of the Celtic summer that corresponds with our May Day).

Her third stone, **Venus** also fell in this area but was hidden.

Pluto in *Winter* suggests that Terri is trying to hang on to a relationship that has been forced to change by her decision to move out of her marriage and home. This has obviously been a source of bereavement to her daughter who was close to both parents. It is likely that Terri's daughter is trying to say to her that things cannot be as they were before.

Mars holds a vital clue to the problems. Terri has been afraid to deal with her daughter's and her own negative feelings, anger, guilt and betrayal. This will have to be acknowledged and dealt with if she is to see her daughter again, however painful it may be. *Spring* suggests these natural hurts stand in the way of a new beginning.

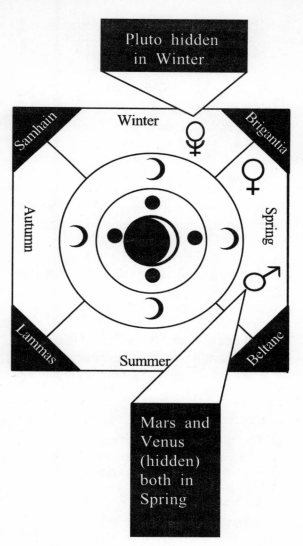

Pluto hidden
in Winter

Mars and
Venus
(hidden)
both in
Spring

Venus, the stone of relationships, confirms
that Terri will need to build a new relationship
with her daughter who may feel doubly be-

trayed: firstly by her mother's departure and secondly by the new family that Terri is mothering.

Sophie may feel she is being disloyal to her father if she sees Terri or acknowledges her new partner. It will need patience and good will on both sides if there is to be any new kind of relationship between Sophie, her mother and perhaps step-brothers and sisters.

Undertakings in the Spring may not be fulfilled till Autumn, perhaps not even then.

Terri was disappointed. She'd wanted reassurance that it would all turn out well. But if we do hurt those we love then we can't expect magic to put it right automatically.

The choice of the *Fire Festival* cloth was apt, since Terri has many inner changes to make if she is to have the good relationship she wants with her daughter.

Although Terri could see the truth of the reading, she still craved reassurance and decided to consult a well-known professional clairvoyant to see if she could provide good news.

She may well find a fortune-teller to let her off the emotional hook and blame her daughter for the rift. But she would probably do better to donate the money to a charity to assuage her guilt.

You don't have to cast your planet stones on a cloth to tune into lunar magic. If you have a particular goal or problem you need to solve, you can pick five planets stones at random to plan out the best way forward.

The stones are laid out in a pathway with Stone One at the bottom to represent the Present Position or Root of the Matter. Above it, place Stone Two for the Goal or End Result. Between them place Stone Three for the Obstacles that you need to remove; Stone Four for Unexpected Influences and Stone Five for Action that will help you to reach the Goal. So your path will look like this:

Stone Two: the Goal.

Stone Five: the Action.

Stone Four: Unexpected Influences.

Stone Three: Obstacles to be overcome.

Stone One: Present position or Root of the Matter.

Think of a question or of your present position, then decide upon a goal. Pick your five stones one at a time, without looking, from your bag. Lay them in a vertical row, putting Stone Two, the Goal, at the top so that you start with a question (Stone One) and finish with the point you're aiming for, (Stone Two). Use the other three to fill in the steps you'll need to take.

Day 28

A Pathway Reading

Frances's reading

Frances is in her late fifties and has been offered early retirement on good terms. However her only daughter lives in Canada and she fears the long, lonely days ahead.

What Frances wants to know is: should she accept the offer or hang on to a job that is the centre of her world?

Her Present Position,
which is Stone One, is **Saturn**   ♄

Her Goal, Stone Two, a
happy retirement is **Uranus**   ♅

The Obstacle, Stone Three,
is **The Sun**   ☉

Unexpected Influences
her Stone Four, is **Neptune**   ♆

Action, Stone Five, is **Earth**   ⊗

Saturn has Frances hemmed in by limitations, fears of being alone, bored, unwanted. Is this really what is happening or are the fears within her greater than the actual situation really warrants?

Let's go to Stone Three, the Obstacles to happiness, that may be causing much of her unease. The **Sun** may seem a strange obstacle. But it might be suggesting that Frances has concentrated so much on success in her job, that she isn't developing her potential in other areas.

She admitted that since her husband died she had thrown herself into her job, even more so once her only daughter had married and emigrated.

Unexpected Influences, Stone Four, **Neptune,** says she should go with the flow. This didn't make sense till Frances admitted that her daughter had been trying to persuade her for years to go to Canada and help her with the flower farm she and her husband ran.

Frances said she had grown up on a farm and her husband had run a smallholding till his death. She had sold it, unable to bear the memories and had concentrated on her business career.

Action, Stone Five, back to the **Earth** literally? Frances said she did still love gardening and missed the land in her long days moving from hotel to hotel. Early retirement and a move to Canada, or a house with a large garden in this country?

Back to Stone Two, the Goal of a happy retirement. **Uranus** says the change wasn't of Frances's making, but if she accepts the ending of her business career, it can free her to develop this other side of herself, that over the years has been pushed aside and almost forgotten in the race for achievement.

You must make the magic!

The Moon Path Reading is not a fortune telling device. What is does to is alert us to a possible path to happiness which we then can take or ignore.

Unlike visiting a clairvoyant who may promise you all manner of goodies in love, success and career, Moon readings can only show you possibilities and limitations.

Sometimes when people phone me on a radio programme and are sick, worried out of their minds by financial problems, or praying that a wandering lover will return, it's very tempting to foretell a happier future just to make them feel better. But happiness can only come sometimes from accepting that a lot of days and effort will pass before the sun shines again.

I know that from my own life and do hope against hope that a surprise cheque will arrive or that someone will whisk me away to the Bahamas from the mountains of washing. But I know the only person who will take me there is me.

The Mood Stones

You now have four pebbles left. These are the mood stones, based on the old alchemists' idea of the four elements: *Earth, Air, Fire* and *Water*. Science has taught us, of course, that these are not really elements but the old ideas are useful to us in a psychological sense.

Day 30

The Mood Stones

You won't throw them on the Moon Cloth but take one out of a separate bag, purse or any small container each morning after you've picked your stone of the day. They can also be useful after you've cast three or six stones on the cloth to tell you how to tackle the problem.

Again, just take one out and note it in your Moon Diary. It will tell you what is the best way to approach your current situation. For example, there are times when we need to follow our gut feeling and empathise with others, and occasions where only a good dose of logic will do.

Deep down we have an instinctive ability to choose the right approach but our judgment can get clouded by our fears and an emphasis on conscious choice (which, of course, isn't really conscious at all but influenced by all kinds of hidden issues).

I haven't used the traditional triangle shapes for the elements because they are very similar and what they mean depends on which way up they land. Instead I've used very simple representations of creatures or symbols associated with each element.

Earth

We have already met **Earth** the planet stone which, in our readings, can indicate the real world and sometimes our failure to relate to life as it is, rather than the way we would like it to be.

I have drawn *Earth* the element as a snake swallowing its own tale, a symbol out of alchemy and Norse legend. It could equally have been another earth symbol such as an elephant, a deer, a horse or unicorn but this is much easier to draw — of course, you can make your snake far more elaborate than mine if you have the skill.

The snake, or serpent, is seen in many cultures as representing the regenerative energy of the soil and guarded it against those who sought to misuse it.

Our *Earth* element represents a practical approach to problems and suggests that, whatever the stumbling block, you are looking at the nitty gritty of who does what and who pays for it. We are dealing with all the mundane things of life from, the toilet rolls to the mortgage; with how you get from A to B and who makes the coffee. But it is vital to get these bricks and mortar issues right, if we are to have a secure base from which to make the intuitive leaps. Someone's got to sort out the things of the flesh of course. But if women are not careful, they end up doing all the slogging and getting very little of the glory.

The *Earth* Element stone differs from the **Earth** Planet Stone, which deals with trusting the evidence of your eyes and ears rather than what others tell you is the truth. But they are linked since both involve going back to brass tacks.

There are all kinds of links between the Planet Stones and the Elements. I'll mention the connections because often, if you get a Planet and Element stone pushing the same message, it's one that should be heeded.

If you pick the Element *Earth,* you may be feeling frazzled and sweeping up at midnight (that was where the book began as Ms Career Girl was frantically cleaning up the flat for Mr Executive's mum's inspection).

The practical hassles of life may be taking away the energy that you need to fulfil your destiny and building up a whole load of resentment that can sour even the most romantic of encounters.

Someone isn't doing his/her share at home or work so it's time for you to draw up rotas and plans. That way you get your time in the sun and don't end up as backroom girl for everyone else's finest hour.

Now let's take a look at what part Earth the element played in someone else's life.

Gill's reading

Gill is in her late fifties and married with two children at home and a grandchild whom she is helping to bring up, as her daughter is a single parent. Gill wants to retire to Spain with her husband next year but he says they can't leave the family. The family agree, although both children seem to have spare money while Gill is struggling. Her son still expects his washing and cooking to be done by mum, although he comes and goes without any warning.

Seeking advice, Gill draws *Earth* the element. Clearly it isn't Gill who needs organising, but ultimately she is going to have to come up with practical solutions if she is literally going to have her place in the Sun.

So how can her oversized baby birds manage without her? Finding accommodation isn't easy for young adults these days. But as long as Gill provides cheap bed and board, no one is going to make any effort to find alternatives.

So Gill has got to start now, steering her

unmarried daughter towards organising accommodation for herself and her little girl. The local council will help single parents. Then Gill must encourage her son to rent or buy a bedsit or flat for himself.

This may involve a crash course in budgeting and upping the rates at home for both children who have been enjoying an easy ride. The kids must also face the ultimate shock of Gill putting her own home on the market. She can also be less available for baby-sitting to encourage her daughter to join forces with other women in her position for work and social cover.

Of course Gill won't abandon her grandchild and will probably end up subsidising trips over to Spain. But if Gill doesn't organise the nitty-gritty of the move now and steer her husband towards a life independent of the children, she may never go and end up feeling very old and bitter.

For *Air* the most obvious symbol is the bird. The mythical thunderbird of the North American Indians who lived by the Great Lakes controlled clouds, rain, thunder and lightning.

Air the Element

The Native American designs were extremely elaborate, differing from tribe to tribe. My bird is a little more basic, a head and lines for the wings but you may draw all kinds of airy creatures on your stone: a dove if you are

Air the Element

feeling peaceable or the eagle, symbol of power and wisdom.

A dose of *Air* tells us that it's no use producing a lot of hot air, tears or threats that we won't carry through. Instead, we need to think hard about what we want and how we can get it. Then we've got to ask quite firmly and be prepared to back up any threats.

As resolute action is needed it is not surprising that **Mars** is the Planet Stone linked with the *Air* element.

If you pick out the *Air* stone, then you may be feeling anything but logical. Throwing a wobbler won't help, however justified it may be, because people will label you hormonal, illogical — you know the names — and make absolutely no concessions once the tears are dried.

Sit down and write out your objectives and ways to achieve them, crossing out any that aren't possible within the law, or those that you know you won't carry through.

For example, if your mother cries every time you mention moving in with your boyfriend and you know you end up crying too and giving way, then you've got to decide logically if you do really want to go (maybe deep down you don't, which will solve the dilemma).

But if you do want to go, how can you achieve

your aim? Accepting that there isn't a painless way and that emotional blackmail is always a killer, you may have to just walk out of that door and not look back.

Sophie's reading
Sophie is in her late twenties and works in an office of chauvinists who insist on treating her as a cross between their mother and the office bimbo, although she is the most highly qualified and competent member of the team.

An Air
reading

She is expected to make coffee, buy sandwiches and her ideas are treated patronisingly, though they are often adopted, usually without crediting her. Now there is a chance for one member to go forward for training for high level management.

Sophie feels confident that she could come through with flying colours. But her superior says it's not worth her putting her name forward as she'll only leave to have babies.

Sophie often goes home in tears and is wondering if they are right about her.

She draws *Air* the element. But venting hot air is the last thing she should do. Logic and firm action are needed. So first she needs to put in that application in spite of what anyone says. Higher up the organisation may be more female friendly and listing her considerable qualifications will increase her confidence in her own worth, as well as sharply reminding her boss and colleagues that she is no bimbo but a very capable woman.

As for the coffee making and sexist remarks, she has to resist accepting this treatment and half-coming to believe the biased assessment of her juvenile colleagues. Of course it's not easy and eventually Sophie may decide to look for another job. But with her new assertiveness she may well get that promotion.

Day 34

Fire the Element

Fire is associated with the salamander (a six-legged lizard) or a fire breathing dragon. But I've chosen a simple horizontal line as the grate with three 60 degree lines above it for the flames. Draw whichever symbol you prefer.

Fire is the inspiration element that provides an alternative solution to the cage of bears or pit of snakes. It draws heavily upon the magic that comes, not from deep within you, but off the top of your head.

Fire is linked with the **Sun** in all its best, most creative aspects, plus the lateral thinking of **Uranus.**

This element indicates that you've reached a crossroads and don't fancy either path on offer. Don't settle for second best. Rearrange the pieces of the jigsaw puzzle that life has set you and see if a third unrecognised solution presents itself. If this new answer comes into your head unbidden, then go for it and worry about the logistics afterwards.

But if the solutions others put forward don't feel right and an alternative doesn't suggest itself, then insist on more time. Go right away from the problem, if only for a walk by yourself, and don't consciously think about the issue. You may even need to sleep on it. The answer will come either in your dreams or daydreams if you listen.

Day 35

A Fire Element reading

Flo's reading

Flo is in her late sixties and has recently married for the second time after being a widow for five years. After the honeymoon, her charming suitor rapidly turned into old Father Traditionalist, who expects his meals cooked and his wife waiting with slippers and cocoa to do his bidding.

When Flo objects, he says she can either 'shut up or ship out'. This is not easy since she has sold her home.

Flo draws *Fire* the element, walks out of the latest quarrel and goes for a long bus ride. On her return she does not make peace with her husband, which, in the past, has meant accepting the blame for everything and promising to try harder in future.

Instead, to his, and particularly to her own,

surprise, she says that she is accepting his invitation to ship out. She will be going to stay with her sister in New Zealand for three months, using a recently matured insurance policy which her husband had earmarked for a joint cruise.

In so many cases I never find out how the story ends as the people I meet by chance go off to work out their own destinies. But in this case I discovered how things turned out. I met Flo in the local tearooms a few months later. She looked very happy. A divorce, a new man? Hubby found he didn't like being on his own again and after two months of hurt silence wrote begging Flo to come home on any terms. And though leopards don't usually change their spots — especially mangy old ones — he is now 'a new man'.

For *Water* you can either draw a fish or, as I have to match my fiery artwork, a more abstract design of three wavy lines. *Water* the element is closest to the watery planet of **Neptune**. Like the Planet stone, it suggests that a sensitive approach is needed and that your feelings may be the best guide to what is really going on.

Water the Element

But it is the other watery function that predominates here. It's a time for going with the flow and taking whatever opportunities are being offered or possibilities suggested.

Water can indicate that plans may not be

working out and you feel worried or scared about taking what is on offer. For now, go along with what's on offer. It's not your gut feeling telling you it's wrong but a free-floating 'Oh heck!'

That's not to say that things will be easy. But if you are flexible and adaptable to the problems you'll meet en route, you may be agreeably surprised.

Day 37

A Water Element reading

Debbie's reading

Debbie is in her forties and a long-standing relationship has broken up leaving her life in ruins and all hope of ever having children gone. Her former partner and his wife-to be work in the same firm so she sees them together every day.

Her sister, who lives in Australia, has suggested that Debbie goes out to join her there for a year and helps to run the family business, an adventure holiday scheme for disturbed teenagers.

But Debbie hesitates as she would have to give up a secure job and sell or rent out her flat which she has redecorated and furnished exactly as she wants it.

Debbie picks out *Water* which tells her what she knows deep inside: that it's no use hanging on to the vestiges of security if you dread each day. Of course it's frightening to give up that well-paid job and immaculate — but empty — flat and go to Australia.

There are no guarantees of a handsome Australian sheep farmer or golden career opportunity. But she may find a different kind of happiness if she takes the opportunity before her.

Day 38

Element and Planet Stones

Jane's reading

Jane is a single parent with a young child, living in council accommodation. Her pregnancy cut her schooling short although she did have a promising future.

So now she has been studying for A levels by correspondence course and at last has enough to qualify for a place as a mature student, at a university 200 miles away from her present home.

She really wants to take up the offer but, at the same time, she does not know how she will cope with her three-year-old son, or pay for the university flat during the vacations when her grant runs out.

Her friends say that she should stay put until her son is of school age as she can just about manage for the moment on her state benefits.

Jane decides to combine her daily choice of Planet Stone with an additional Element stone to clarify her thoughts.

Over three days she chooses.

Day 1. **Sun** and *Water*

Day 2. **Sun** and *Fire*

Day 3. **Pluto** and *Water*

The **Sun** represents Jane's chance to make a
better life for herself and, in the long-term, for
her young son. The *Water* stone suggests that
she should take the opportunity which is lying
before her, rather than trying to have cast iron
guarantees about her future or waiting for the
right moment — which never comes.

On the next day the **Sun** appears again, em-
phasising that if she doesn't fulfil her potential,
whatever the hardships, then ultimately she
will resent her child in future for 'holding her
back'. *Fire* reminds her that she can use her

own creative energies to overcome these hard-ships. There may be other avenues she has not explored yet.

On the third day **Pluto** says that it's time for Jane to move on to the next stage of her life. Of course it won't be easy and will involve all kinds of financial and child-care problems that can only be faced one by one as they occur.

But then her present life isn't easy and she certainly won't remain satisfied with it, if she turns this chance down.

The *Water* stone appears for a second time, reminding Jane that if she is flexible and adapt-able, she will find ways round the difficulties of the new situation. For example, it may be possible for her to sort out some form of shared child-care with other students who are in simi-lar situations. Or perhaps she might even make some money in the vacation by looking after the children of other working mothers while she takes care of her own boy.

Start to use the Element Stones each day, either after you have picked out your daily planet stone, or in addition to each reading of three or six stones. If you don't want to use the Element Stones daily but only as a part of a longer reading, that's up to you — there are no rights and wrongs, only what feels best for you. Either way remember to keep these four stones separately from your Planet Stones.

Although I have just said that you should keep the Planet Stones and the Element Stones apart as we cast the Planets and choose the Elements, they can, of course, be used together to give you a deeper insight when you are casting.

If you do a cast of three or six and the solution doesn't seem clear, you can pick an element stone from your bag of four to guide you towards the best path forward. Remember:

A Mixed reading

Earth is for a practical solution;

Air is for a logical path;

Fire is for the off-the-top-of-your-head creativity.

Water is going with the flow and using your gut feelings.

Tanya's reading

Tanya is about to start her own computerised secretarial company with a small business grant. But her husband, Greg, is very worried about her being self-employed as her salary is essential to the family budget if they are to keep paying the mortgage.

Besides, he says, he doesn't want the clutter of her work around the home as he is very

A reading for Tanya

house-proud. But Tanya is tired of working for other people and knows that her skills are very much in demand. Should she go ahead or should she listen to Greg? She casts:

> Stone 1: **Venus** in her inner *Waxing Moon* circle
>
> Stone 2: **Earth** also in her *Waxing Moon* circle
>
> Stone 3: **Mercury** in her outer *Waning Moon* circle

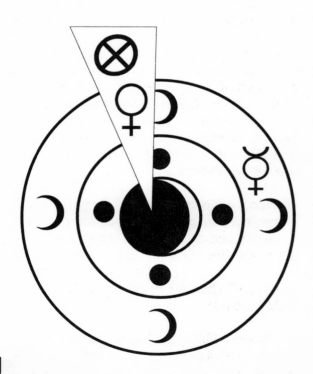

Venus alerts Tanya that her relationship with her husband needs to change if she is to develop her own potential. She said that he came from a home where his mother was always out working and things were a mess, so he has always felt that Tanya should keep the home nicely. So she is seen in the housekeeping role, in spite of her full-time job.

Earth tells her to trust her own common sense and do what she knows is right for her and which she has carefully costed and planned. Her initial grants from the Enterprise Board will cover the mortgage payments till money starts flowing. So this objection isn't sound.

Mercury is perhaps a key. Communication, or lack of it, may be behind Greg's objections. What does he really fear? That Tanya will neglect him as his mother did once her job becomes a business? Can Tanya reassure him without compromising her own independence?

Tanya casts three more stones.

Stone 4: **Neptune** in the outer segment of *Summer,* the *Time of Nurturing.* (Tanya is using the Solar divisions of this outer area).

Stone 5: The **Sun** hidden in the *Full Moon* circle.

Stone 6: The **Blank Planet** in her *Waxing* inner circle.

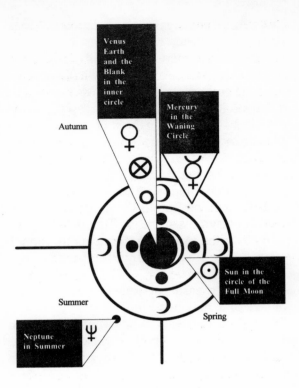

Venus
Earth
and the
Blank
in the
inner
circle

Autumn

Mercury
in the
Waning
Circle

Sun in the
circle of the
Full Moon

Summer

Spring

Neptune
in Summer

A reading for Tanya

Neptune tells Tanya to look below the surface to what Greg is really thinking and not what he is saying. Is he worried about the power structure of the relationship changing and using money and housework as an excuse?

Tanya said that Greg's dad had very much played second fiddle to his mum and had moved out when Greg was quite young. So it's vital to get to the bottom of the real issues that if unresolved may affect other areas of their relationship. Right now Tanya's nurturing qualities are needed if she is to reassure Greg.

The **Sun** is a reminder that, unless Tanya does fulfil her potential, she is going to feel resentful and ultimately may blame Greg if she is stuck in a mould she doesn't want.

The **Blank Planet** in her *Waxing* circle says she should take that new beginning and step into the unknown.

But that leaves us with a dilemma. Tanya needs to follow her dreams if she is to feel really fulfilled. And yet if Greg isn't supportive, it will be very hard for her and she is less likely to succeed. She loves Greg and so ignoring him isn't really an option.

Tanya takes a planet stone from her bag. It is the *Earth* element. As she had already drawn the Planet Stone, **Earth,** it seems that a back to basics, step by step approach is definitely indicated. So did she have a practical 'earthy' alternative? She thought about it and wondered if perhaps she could start her business part-time while taking some temporary jobs, in return for Greg weighing in on the practical front, thus taking the pressure off Tanya to keep things up to scratch.

To her surprise, Greg agreed to help around the house and started to do her book work in the evenings. After a few weeks he suggested she gave up temping and that she expanded into desk-top publishing, with his help, (he was a systems analyst) with the long term view of them working together from home.

An Element Stone can be helpful if a reading is dealing with a complex issue with several strands and can offer a strategy towards tackling a problem from the best angle.

Day 40

A Jungian approach

For a life review or a relationship issue, the Planet Stones can be used to see how the underlying issues affect our conscious decisions. I have called this the Jungian approach after the psychologist, Carl Gustav, Jung, who was fascinated by the relationship between chance with significant incidents in life. You will need to pick five stones and arrange four of them in a square with the fifth in the centre.

Stone 1: The *Archetype* or Predominant Pattern is placed in a 12 o'clock position, to the North. This tells us the overriding theme dominating our life at a particular point. You may find that one particular Planet Stone often occupies this position. This reflects another Jungian aspect of being, the face we show the world.

Stone 2: The *Animus* is placed in the 3 o'clock position to the East. This deals with the competitive, go-getting logical side we all have. Sometimes an intuitive, feminine stone appears which says that we may be blocking our own positive approach because we feel it's

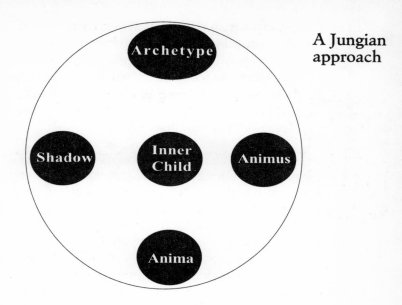

not right to be assertive.

Stone 3: The *Anima,* is placed in the 6 o'clock or South position and talks of our intuitive, caring side that is as vital in men as well as women if we are to fulfil our whole selves. A logical, masculine stone here can say we're trying to apply logic to a situation of the heart.

Stone 4: The *Shadow* is placed in the 9 o'clock or West position and speaks of our negative emotions that we often deny or project on to others. But which can, if properly channelled, be a powerful impetus to action and positive change.

Stone 5: The *Inner Child,* goes in the centre

of the other four stones and is the combination and synthesis of all these aspects. It shows us the best path to take to fulfil our unique potential. Often, this stone is completely different from the one which you may have been expecting. But subsequent events usually prove that it was the only one possible.

You may not like this way of using the stones and do not need to try it unless you wish. For many people a cast of three or six planet stones on the Moon Cloth answers issues on all levels, especially when used in conjunction with a mood stone.

But I have found a Jungian reading very useful at a time when I've needed an in-depth consideration of where I'm going. It's not a reading to be done in a hurry, so be quiet and alone and make this time special to you.

A Jungian reading

Patricia's reading

Patricia is in her late forties and married to John who is twenty five years older and was her boss. They never had children and in the fifteen years they have been together they have rarely been apart. Now he has retired and her new boss Ken is about her own age and great fun to work with. John is urging her to give up work so they can retire to the South Coast but she feels she will be buried alive.

Since his retirement John has aged rapidly and usually dozes off during the early evening, leaving her alone in front of the television. Ken, who is separated from his wife, has suggested they meet after work for a meal to discuss future projects. Patricia is tempted as she knows Ken is interested in her as a woman and has hinted there might be trips to Paris and Amsterdam, with her as his special assistant.

Patricia hadn't used the Planet Stones before and didn't want to use the cloth. She picked five planet stones from my bag.

> **Stone 1**: **Jupiter** represented the *Predominant Archetype* or pattern in her life. This went in the 12 o'clock position.

> **Stone 2:** The **Sun** stood for her *Animus* or assertive aspect and went in a 3 o'clock position.

> **Stone 3: Pluto** was her *Anima* or nurturing side and went in the 6 o'clock position.

> **Stone 4: Venus** was her *Shadow* or negative feelings and went in the 9 o'clock position.

> **Stone 5:** The **Moon** was her *Inner Child* or true self and went in the centre of the reading.

Jupiter represents the conventional nature of Patricia's life, safe if dull, that, until now, has

A reading for Patricia

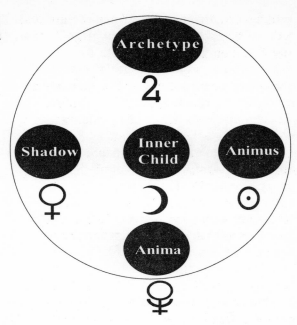

satisfied her. But with her husband's retirement comes the realisation that the age gap is there. Often it is not until one partner shows signs of ageing that a difference in years becomes acutely noticeable.

And retirement has been a big change point both for Patricia and John — even more for her than for him.

The **Sun** speaks of Patricia's own desire not 'to be buried alive' in her husband's withdrawal from the working world. But another man may not be the answer. There are still many ways she can fulfil her own working potential and perhaps help to keep her husband by encouraging John to start new projects now he is free from a work timetable.

Pluto may seem a strange planet to represent her *Nurturing* role but it suggests that she has got into a rut as the receptive partner and that this stage may be redundant. The last two stones hint that the wise, dominant older man and passive, younger wife roles may be changing and while this is not easy at any change point, she may now be the one to develop her career. She may need to leave her present job, not necessarily to retire but to find a new path for herself.

Venus as her *Shadow* says that another relationship, again boss and assistant, isn't the answer. Instead she needs to find a new way of relating to her husband within the marriage, or ultimately accepting it has run its course. She's repressing a lot of resentment and uncertainties so she needs to sort out her present situation before considering another.

She may, for years, have been growing less happy with the daddy/little girl scenario. The retirement issue may give her a chance to change the power structure in the relationship (as shown by the *Animus* and *Anima* stones).

Finally, the **Moon** is her *Inner Child*, which is very different from the daughter role she has occupied in her marriage. It says she should use her intuition and unconscious wisdom to guide her and John to a future that may suit them both, rather than labour under the illusion of romantic escapes which can only lead to heartache.

Patricia said the stones echoed her growing realisation that she should resign from her job before things got out of hand. The **Sun** stone had reminded her that she and her husband had always talked of opening a cafe when he retired. Perhaps they should rekindle the dream.

Day 42

The last day

And that is the Moon Magic divination system for you to adapt to your own lifestyle. We cannot and should not give up our solar clock. At its best the oomph and wider timescale enable us to fulfil our creative and logical sides.

But just as important, though not recognised by the logic of our left-brained society, is the intuitive cyclical flow that helps women to live by their own ebbs and flows and not the ticking of the clock.

Moon divination is perhaps the magic closest to women's own natural powers because the gentle, intuitive wisdom of the moon mirrors our own rich inner world.

The legends of those days of a woman-centred ancient society, passing its gentle life under the rule of the White Goddess, may be nothing more than a myth. But, as with all legends, it does have a kernel of truth. Women are special and have a unique beauty at whatever age or stage they may be passing through.

The lesson of the moon is to live fully through each of these stages — even the dark stage of the *Waning Moon*. For if we try to hang on to a redundant stage and go against the natural tides, it is inevitable that we will experience conflict and a sense of failure.

Moon Magic reminds us that there really is a time for everything. When the outer world fails us, we can move back to our own inner sanctuary of a slower pace and know that soon we will enter another cycle.

There are many new moons, many chances to start again.

Equally, those periods will come when we have the energy to go for broke and the confidence to go out and make our mark on the world. And when we are tired, then the waning moons give us permission to rest and be still in the knowledge that enthusiasm will return and we can begin anew.

That is the real magic of the moon and harnessing those natural times can give us the edge over those who live only by the solar clock.

Moon Divination, which charts your inner stars (as opposed to the horoscopes of far-off stars), can offer a way of seeing your life in a different time scale and being aware of the

The Natural Power of the Moon unconscious factors that may push you into one course rather than another which, left to yourself, you might have chosen.

If you can read your stones by moonlight at each of the lunar phases, then you can feel those deep energies stirring within you. But even though life is often less than ideal you know that whether in moonlight, sunlight or on the greyest day, your lunar inner sights and powers will create a magic that cannot be extinguished.

Any magic is only as good as the effort you make in the earthly plane to make it happen and any divination can only point to possible courses or paths. Only you can tread them or decide to turn away.

But that is what makes *Today's Woman* magic so special. Because it makes no false promises or sets up impossible goals, you can make it come true. If in doubt look at the moon and don't just make a wish — make sure your dreams come true.

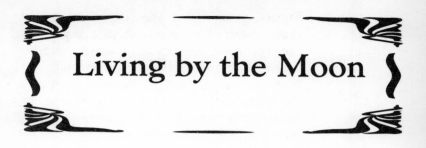

Living by the Moon

Moon divination is a special way of getting in touch with our inner world. But there are other ways in which women can use the rhythms of the Moon to harmonise and regulate their worlds. Many women find that the softer light of Moon Magic, even more than astrology, reflects their unique inner path to spirituality.

Its phases of Maiden, Mother and Wise Woman, that I talked of in the first chapter, mirror the natural stages of growth, fruition and maturity that must be lived through and left behind at the right moment.

The *Waxing* first phase, the phase of the Maiden, which is strongest on the day of the New Moon and the following week, sees a woman setting new goals however small. Initiating both spiritually and practically, new directions in her life. However, she may need many new moons before she can see progress towards her goals.

Some women find it helpful to meet to light candles on the New Moon and collectively focus their needs. But you can equally well do it alone, using light clear colours that you feel are right, not those that have been set down by others. It's a time for early morning walks, for buying herbs or planting things, for writing those letters you've been putting off and for making those phone calls, especially if they will lead to wider opportunities.

The *Full Moon* period is the time of maximum power when the woman can put all her energies into action, push herself to the limit, make those leaps and succeed. It is a time of confidence and a good time for crystal work. You can surround all your favourite crystals with bright candles, fill vases with bright flowers, leaves or berries.

Or you can try filling your bath with coloured fragrances. It's a time to wear bright colours and meet people head on.

The *Waning Phase* is not wasted. It is a time for inner creation, for banishing the outworn and negative aspects of life and for closing down the outward focus and claiming the inner peace from which all magic flows.

Make a nothing time each day, even for just 10 minutes, for you alone. Surround yourself with soft lights or candles, warm duvets and big cushions. Tape up the doorbell and take the phone off the hook — the world will always come back if it's important. It's a time to be alone, not with tapes of waterfalls or bird song unless you really want them. Otherwise, just let the images flow free. If past lives come, let them.

You may want to drop scented oil in water or make sand pictures. You may want to pick up brown pebbles, take them home and feel the receptive energy absorbing your pain and sorrow. In the last days of the *Dark of the Moon* let the regrets of the month flow.

Have a good cry if you feel like it. There's a new moon coming and you can start again. You may like to burn the incense of the Moon, jasmine.

The Moon and your body

On a smaller scale women can see the cyclic pattern of the moon in the monthly menstrual cycle. It can be very difficult to reconcile menstruation with all the demands of working life and it seems as if at least for a few days a month guys have the advantage.

But while male hormones are less cyclical, their biological drives don't have the rhythmic flow that women can utilise to tap into differing approaches.

Even PMT can be a way of telling us to rest, slow down and retreat to let our spirit draw strength from quiet and contemplation. For women with physical fertility, as opposed to the psychic fertility of the later years, it may be possible to gradually bring the menstrual cycle

The Moon and your body

into line with the Moon, so that we bleed during the five days called the Dark of the Moon. These come at the end of the waning phase and until the New Moon is visible in the sky. In this way we harness the positive aspects of the Dark of the Moon and are able to draw on lunar energies.

Women in boarding schools, or colleges or even close friends, do find that their menstrual cycles coincide. In drawing on our natural inner magic the Moon's phases can help us to focus on different kinds of power available to us.

It has been believed that the Moon flowed as the wise blood of the Goddess in women. In primitive times women withdrew to special huts to harness the dark power of the moon when they menstruated.

So first chart your menstrual cycle with that of the lunar month. You may be surprised how closely they align and as your moon magic work continues, your menstrual clock may be automatically adjusting.

For the woman who no longer menstruates it is even easier to live by the lunar phases. This may explain a lot of so-called misplaced hormonal reactions that are simply your body's way of saying it's time to slow down. If your monthly clock does widely differ from moon time take it gently, go with what your body is saying and let your inner Moon pattern guide you.

We don't have time that our ancestors did to follow the gentle pace of the Moon. If we're racing against the solar clock, it's not surprising what's happening in the sky isn't totally in sync with our inner world.

So draw up your own Moon time in your Moon Diary if you are still of child-bearing years and, for now, just note any similarities with the Moonclock. Try to fit in your monthly timetable with your own ebbs and flows, not easy. Towards the end of menstruation you may begin to feel enthusiastic and very receptive in a gentle way.

It's a good time in your monthly cycle to concentrate on negotiations or dealing with new material or people, because you are receptive and ready to compromise and be patient. For me it's a time to book up radio shows or send out proposals.

At ovulation, you may feel a slight pain or just a heightened awareness and so it's a time to really meet any problems head on. Put in the extra hours or get ahead, whether with chores or work, so that you can free-wheel later in the month. It's a time I work towards deadlines and cram a week into every day.

As you move into your premenstrual period, however long it is, you can actually harness the restlessness and rattiness to do those jobs you hate. If you're feeling miserable any way, you might as well do the things that make you unhappy. As they have to be done anyway, why do them when you're in a good mood and spoil that time?

But go easy. It's a time for small, regular carbohydrate meals to stop you bingeing. If you aren't still menstruating, then begin your month with the New Moon but be flexible about when your phases change. If you're still at full power as the Moon begins to wane, go with your inner clock till you feel the power beginning to wane or you start to feel ratty and know you are pushing yourself too hard.

When you begin to menstruate, be kind to yourself. Of course you've still got to work and carry out the thousand and one tasks of your life. But if you've got ahead in the mid-cycle then you can take the odd early night off, relax and be aware of the power of your woman-hood.

In Tantric and some ancient nature religions a woman's menstruation was something to be celebrated as symbol of her creative power. But too often society has that Old Testament idea that menstruation is unclean and even the most liberated guy can have that primitive reaction and be a bit nervous of you.

So educate any men around you who start cracking daft jokes or backing off and help them to understand your monthly cycle. Make them aware that you're not a raging bag of hormones to be avoided at all costs but that your energy levels do change and that if you are feeling premenstrual, you don't want to be handled like a sack of potatoes.

The Moon and children

When I was a child I used to stand in my Birmingham back-yard, bow to the New Moon and turn over a sixpence. To children, the Moon is very magical and whether you live in a high rise block or by the sea, the Moon's phases are equally vivid.

Children may like to chart the Moon's progress. Most newspapers have the daily changes in the moon that children can copy or paste into a book.

You may find that babies, toddlers and adolescents of both sexes have a cyclic flow. Toddler tantrums may be partly due to a child pushing ahead when he or she is tired, or from being expected to sit quietly at a time of full energy.

With children of any age, you can harness their natural ebbs and flows. A New Moon phase can be utilised with an activity that involves exploring a new place or starting a new activity. Because it's quite a gentle phase, children can be especially receptive to animals and nature. It's not a time for adventure playgrounds or action-packed days of running round filling every moment with frantic activity.

The Moon and children When the Full Moon energies flow, it is a time for that trip round the museum or to a safari park, although activities that cost a lot aren't always those that are best enjoyed. A long walk, or a day trying out the activities at the local park or sports centre, can be appreciated and harness those energies that can easily be diverted into mischief or boredom if untapped.

The Waning phase may, if unheeded, lead to tantrums, sulks or even hyperactivity. Many children even into adolescence need help in quietening themselves and resting. So it's not a time to complain about untidy rooms.

Allow extra time for everything. Losing games kit and homework is something that is inbuilt into children and you are always ready to cope with that. But in the Waning phase you're lucky if they remember their heads, let alone their caps and coats.

Try to spend time as a family with familiar meals and quiet activities keeping TV to a minimum. And don't forget the cuddles. Children can also become aware of the physical magic of the moon.

Going out at night, even if it is only into the garden, at Full Moon and seeing how light the world is on a clear night provides a link with an earlier world where people rose and went to bed by the Sun and were grateful for the light of the Moon. It can be fun on holiday to live by the Sun and Moon for a day and night, especially if you are camping. But it's possible anywhere.

Let children put crystals on the window ledge and see the difference between reflected moonlight as opposed to sunlight. Explain the moon is there even if they can't see it. On a clear night of a Full Moon, some children who are afraid of the dark can begin to realise that darkness isn't bad or scary but the other half of existence.

If you can, visit a planetarium or museum that has a section on astronomy (the Natural History Museum in London is well worth a visit). Even young children pick up a remarkable amount of information (my six-year-old can now pick out Orion's head, 'Beetlejuice'). It's a wonderful way of getting the material world into perspective, with all those glowing stars millions of light years away.

Your day and night cycle also operates on the triple lunar system. For a week or so, chart your natural highs and lows of energy and enthusiasm.

Of course, you can't have a nap at noon if you're in the middle of a board meeting or have got to get lunch for three fractious toddlers. But if you are aware of being in a waning phase when you should be up and running, then you can use odd moments to switch off and build up strength for when you've simply got to be on top form. You can then either do the necessary spadework or polish off the details when you are feeling humming with energy.

But unlike more conventional ideas of bio-rhythms, just as the New Moon comes at different days on different months, you can subtly and gradually alter your daily lunar clock. So, if you've got small children who are up with the lark, you adapt your ebbs and flows to fit with them — your waxing phase starts at five and you're tucked up with your hot water bottle and sloppy novel (or man) at nine.

Adapt to the most overriding need or needs of your life when full peak energy is essential, remembering you can't go from stop to full power.

A lot of us miss out the waxing phase in our day and by the time we're feeling in top form the cleaners are dusting round our desk and we're scowling over the brilliant remark we didn't make.

Equally we need to have a waning period. Otherwise we end up with insomnia as we re-run the day's failures and tomorrow's potential disasters through into the small hours.

The old fashioned slippers and cocoa routine masked a very common sense winding down phase.

I know that when I end up running round with the vacuum cleaner in the evening when I should be concentrating on the bed-time story.

The children go to bed hyped up, I end up yelling and no one wanes gradually and sinks into sleep.

All very well you say, going with the natural rhythms but the kids are up at five and I'm an Owl and need my sleep. The Owl/Lark theory is a bit of a blind alley because it implies we are what we are and can't change, even if red hot pincers are applied to our favourite teddy.

What is more, it's not strictly true. Some species of owls fly all day and sleep all night. It's all a matter of priorities and if your particular prey is only around between ten and four in the afternoon then that's when you get out there, talons poised, if you're going to stave off the bank manager.

It is easier than it sounds to move your waning period round so you're ready for battle at noon. Get up really early for a few mornings even if you have to prop your eyelids open with matchsticks. Then you'll be glad to go to bed early. Keep up the routine even at weekends. Cities in the early morning are remarkably lovely and you'll be first at the shops or the theme park.

Gradually you'll find you are living a different way and don't waste your energy feeling tired or hard-done by. And so the solar dash becomes more manageable when mediated by the Moon, just as the harsh world dissolves and becomes more magical by night when touched by moonbeams.

We are creatures of the Moon, mysterious, intuitive, creative.

On the surface we may be jostled by the pace of modern day living. But, like our ancestors who observed the phases of the Moon from their cave, we know that deep down we respond to an inner flow. Look up at the night sky even if it is cloudy. The Moon is there and promises that each month we can start again with renewed energy and the slate wiped clean.

The Moon reminds us that we are very special, magical whether in meditation or sweeping up yesterday's corn flakes and we can fulfil our dreams if we just hold faith. Happy Monday.

As with all spells, Moon Magic galvanises your own energies so you've always got to follow through with action in the real world.

How to wish on the Moon

A New Moon Money Spell. Stand in the garden and hold a silver coin in your right hand (for action in the real world) while chanting:

New Moon,

True Moon,

Star in the stream.

Bring me fortune in my dream.

Place the money under your pillow and you will dream of how to improve your fortunes. Next morning take the first steps towards fulfilling your plan, however small.

A love spell

This can be performed at the Full Moon. Stand in the garden or at an open window and visualise the one you want to love you. Then recite:

I gaze at the Moon,

The Moon sees me,

The Moon brings (his name)

Here to me.

You may then write your loved one's name on a stone and place it on the window ledge till the Moon begins to wane. Meanwhile, arrange to see him and work your own magic.

For kicking a bad habit

This spell, which is said to be equally effective for getting rid of the negative influence of someone who is dragging you down, should be performed at the time of the Waning Moon.

Lady Moon, give me power,

To be more happy by the hour,

To love myself and leave behind,

The sorrows that to weakness bind.

Either write the name of what or who you want to give up on a stone and bury it in the earth or throw it into running water. If you remove something you must always replace it, so plant seeds over the stone, take up a new activity or go to a new place the next day.

These are just suggestions. You can perform your own rituals and spells in accordance with the phases of the moon. But remember never to use your magic to wish anyone harm or try for money or love by dubious means.

It always rebounds, at the best psychologically, at the worst who knows. And only you can make those wishes come true ultimately by your own earthly efforts.

Moon lore

The day of the Moon is Monday, the angel of the Moon is Gabriel, its Zodiacal sign Cancer (June 21-July 20).

Its element is water, its colour silver, its metal silver, its stone the moonstone that some say gets brighter in the first phase, is brightest at Full Moon and then gets paler. Its flower is night-scented sock, its animals the dog and crab and its bird the owl.

The old superstitions tell us that:

You must plant during the growing Moon and not the waning.

Cut your hair at the New Moon and it will grow thick and glossy.

If you point at the Moon, you won't go to heaven.

The best marriages begin at Full Moon.

A child born at the Full Moon will be strong.

A robbery committed on the third day of the New Moon will fail.

The Moon with a circle brings water in her beak. A single misty ring around the Moon means rain or snow.

If the Full Moon rises red, it will be windy.

To dream of the Moon is said to foretell unexpected joy and success in love.

A New Moon is said to be good for tradesmen, farmers and lovers (which is good news for shopkeepers who want to sow their wild oats).

The Full Moon denotes marriage and is said to shine especially benignly on widows.

Moon lore

To dream of the waning Moon foretells the end of a difficult period in your life.

To see the New Moon on a Monday signifies good luck and good weather.

The New Moon seen for the first time over the right shoulder says that whatever you wish will come true.

If you look at the New Moon through glass your wish will be delayed (so take off your glasses and open the window before the Moon rises).

Turning silver over at the time of the New Moon means that your cash flow will increase by the end of the month (unfortunately I never seem to have any silver to turn over at the time of the New Moon — or any other).

Summary

The Hidden Message of the Planet Stones

You will only mark one side of your planet stones. But if you throw your stone face down, it is as significant as if your stone lands marked side up. Turn it over very gently and see what it is you are holding back.

The Planet Stones.

The **Sun**: If you get the **Sun** Stone in a reading then you may be faced with a new opportunity or direction. Go for it.

When the **Sun** is hidden, you may be encouraging those closest to you to live out your dreams. It's never too late to reach the goal yourself.

The **Moon:** If you get the **Moon** in a reading then you are overdosing on logic and other people's advice. Trust your inner wisdom.

When your **Moon** sign is hidden you may be tempted to take the line of the least resistance. But if you hand over your future for others to make, that can only bring pain in the long run.

The **Earth:** If you get the **Earth** stone in a reading, you may be ignoring your own common sense which will help you to see through jargon to the real situation.

When the **Earth** Stone is hidden you may be feeling out of touch with the real world. Sort out who and what really matter to you.

Mercury: If you get **Mercury** in a reading, then there's something you need to communicate. But it's important to be sure you express yourself clearly and listen to what the other person is really saying in return.

When **Mercury** is hidden, then most of the communication is taking place in your head. Don't anticipate defeat or worse still be so exhausted or dispirited with the inner rehearsal you don't bother.

Venus: If you get **Venus** in a reading then relationships are the name of the game and you may find yourself placating friends and family at the expense of your own peace of mind. Let others take their share of responsibility for good relations.

If **Venus** is hidden, then it might be that you are looking at people in terms of the roles they occupy and not whether you like them or approve of their actions.

Treat them as individuals and demand that same respect in return.

Mars: If you get **Mars** in a reading, you are probably feeling flaming mad, or at least pretty resentful about the status quo. So it's time to state quite clearly your grievances. Sometimes you've got to tread on a few toes, if your feelings aren't to be trampled on or eroded.

When **Mars** is hidden, then you're using a lot of energy keeping the lid on your feelings. Stop the twenty-four-hours-a-day smile when you feel like yelling.

Jupiter: If you get **Jupiter** in a reading, then the chances are you're not going to get in by the back door, or by one of those inspirational leaps, but by following the conventional path. For once, do it by the book.

When **Jupiter** is hidden, it may be indicating that you have been taking one chance too many because you've been lucky in the past. Be careful not to get too maverick.

Saturn in a reading means you're letting the past dominate the present and old resentments and regrets may be stopping you making the most of the benefits of here and now. Go from where you are now not where you wish you'd been.

When **Saturn** is hidden you may be playing that old guilt harp yourself and loading on to others your own lack of achievement or happiness, something which may not be down to them.

Uranus: If you get **Uranus**, then the old answers don't fit to the new situation or problem and an original approach is needed. So the question is not 'Should I?' but 'How?'

When **Uranus** is hidden, then you're looking at the negative side of the change. Concentrate on the logistics and worry about the metaphysics when you've made the leap.

Neptune: If you get **Neptune** in a reading the surface situation is not what it seems. Tune in to what people mean and feel and not what they say or do.

When **Neptune** is hidden you may be riding high emotionally and dreaming of bunnies, red hearts and roses. But don't get carried away by sentiment or illusions. Listen to your gut feeling and read the small print.

Pluto: If you get **Pluto** in a reading then you may be at a natural change point. We cannot open new doors until we've said goodbye to the old way of life. So be brave and set your sights on the next part of the journey.

When **Pluto** is hidden then we're actually planning a backward step to stop us confronting the real issue.

Whatever the backward step, ask yourself why you are taking it and be sure it is really what you want.

The Moon Cloth.

The inner circle is the area of the *New* and *Waxing Moon* and of new beginnings. Stones that fall in this circle are rooted in the initial enthusiasms and uncertainties, so you may be feeling a bit vulnerable as well as excited. But each step, however faltering, is a positive one.

The middle circle is the circle of the *Full Moon* when full power is available and full effort demanded. Be confident that, whatever the issue, you've got the wherewithal to carry it through and you are definitely on the right track. So don't be fobbed off or persuaded to settle for second best.

The third circle is that of the *Waning/Dark of*

the Moon. So it's a good time for getting rid of the chaff and preparing the ground for those new beginnings (the Moon cycle). It's not a destructive time but one for recognising that there is a time and a season for every purpose under heaven.

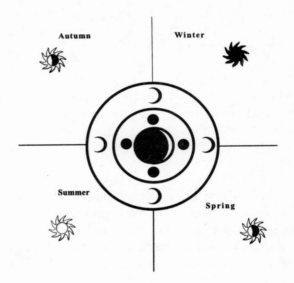

The Outer Segments

On my cloth, stones that fall into the outer segment between March 21 and June 21 (March 21 starts at the 3 o'clock equivalent on the clock) are in the *Spring* segment.

Spring is sometimes called *The Time of Sowing* and whether the calendar on the wall says January or June, when your stone falls here you may find yourself propelled into a new situation not necessarily of your choosing.

The outer segment, between June 21 and September 21, is the *Summer* segment (starting at the 6 o'clock position). *Summer* or *The Time of Nurturing* represents a period when you will be called upon to do the nurturing. Accept that at this phase in your life you may be forced to take on responsibilities and put in a great deal of effort for no immediate benefit.

The outer segment, *Autumn* or *The Time of Gathering*, is the segment between September 21 and December 21 (starting at 9 o'clock). This area involves looking backwards as well as forwards, of assessing your successes and planning your next move.

The fourth outer segment, *Winter* or *The Time of Waiting*, takes us to the top of our clock and we can only hope, whichever gods or goddesses we try to placate, that spring will follow this dismal time of the year and soul.

But dismal or not, winter is a vital season. It is a time in our lives for withdrawing into ourselves and deciding what is important to us deep down.

Casting the Stones
The important thing to remember is that is you should not look at the stones before you pick them, but take them at random from your bag or purse.

Casting the Stones

For a cast of three you may prefer to pick three at a time and throw them in the direction of the cloth.

Some people find it easier to pick them out singly and throw them. But there are no rules carved in stone. The system is yours.

Personally, I find it easier to throw three stones and then read them together rather than reading each one as I throw it. But again, it is entirely up to you.

For a reading of six Planet Stones you can throw all six and read them together. But you may find it easier to cast the first batch of three stones, read them then cast the second set of three and see how they add to what the first batch has told you.

Again, I must stress, that there are no hard and fast rules and you will develop your own way in time.

The Mood Stones

The Mood Stones are based on the old alchemists' idea of the four elements: *Earth, Air, Fire* and *Water*. Although modern science uses different classifications for elements, these ancient ideas represent a useful way of getting in touch with our inner qualities.

You won't throw them on the Moon Cloth. Take one out of a separate bag, purse or any small container each morning after you've picked your stone of the day.

They can also be useful after you've cast three or six stones on the cloth, in offering a way in which you should tackle the problem which your cast of three or six has highlighted.

Deep down, we have an instinctive ability to choose the right approach. But our judgment can get clouded by our fears and an emphasis on conscious choice, which of course isn't really conscious at all but influenced by all kinds of hidden issues.

The *Earth* element represents a practical approach to problems and suggests that, whatever the apparent stumbling block, you are looking at improvements in the everyday organisation of your life for a solution, perhaps getting other people to do a bit more of the slog.

A dose of *Air* tells us that it's no use producing a lot of hot air, tears or threats we won't carry through, but that we need to think hard about what we want and how we can get it.

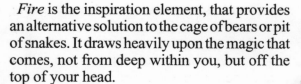

Then we've got to ask quite firmly and be prepared to back up any threats with action.

Fire is the inspiration element, that provides an alternative solution to the cage of bears or pit of snakes. It draws heavily upon the magic that comes, not from deep within you, but off the top of your head.

If a new answer to an old question comes into your head unbidden, go for it and worry about the logistics afterwards.

 Water suggests that a sensitive approach is needed and that your feelings may be the best guide to what is really going on. But it is the other watery function that predominates here.

It's a time for going with the flow and taking whatever opportunities are being offered or possibilities suggested.

An Optional Moon Cloth

This cloth is for when you are thinking of an inner issue or something beyond the everyday world.

The first three circles are the same as the normal cloth: the inner circle is the *Waxing Moon,* the middle circle is the *Full Moon* and the outer circle is the *Waning Moon*. The difference is in the outer circles.

The first segment, *Winter* begins at the north-west compass position and is dated at the evening of November 2. Draw your first winter line about half way between 10 and 11 on a clock face as a diagonal line. The Celtic Winter began at *Samhain* on October 31 and is the equivalent of All Souls' Eve and Hallowe'en.

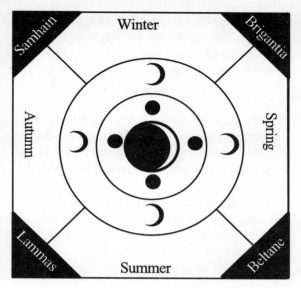

The second segment, *Spring,* begins in the north-east compass position. The fire festival, *Brigantia,* began on January 31. This is marked between 1 and 2 o'clock on a traditional clock face position as a diagonal line.

The third segment, *Summer,* begins in the south-east compass position. The Celtic Summer began on *Beltane*, the Eve of April 30, Draw this line diagonally between 4 and 5 o'clock on a traditional clock face.

The fourth segment, *Autumn*, begins in the south-west compass position. *Lammas*, July 31 marked High Summer. Draw this line diagonally between 7 and 8 o'clock on a traditional clock face. These Fire Festival divisions have exactly the same meanings as the solar

An optional Moon Cloth ones. *Winter* still indicates a time of trust and waiting, *Spring* a time of making new plans and starting new ventures, *Summer* the golden days of your power and nurturing efforts and *Autumn* a time to reap and gather in and assess and start to slow down.

When a stone is hidden (falling face down), it's a time to see what's happening below the surface and what or who is holding you back.

You may find you are making obstacles without realising it. Ask yourself why and if you don't want change right now, accept that you and only you are in control and go with your inner flow, whatever the outside world is screaming or demanding.

But you will find that the obstacles indicated apply to your inner spiritual world rather than actual events or your daily life and relationships. You may wish only to use this cloth for yourself.

Feel free to return to this summary as often as you need to. Remember — you are working towards improving your lifestyle, not towards appearing on Mastermind with Moon Divination as your special subject.

152

Today's Woman Divination series

Each is written in the same easy-to-follow style and, in a six-week course, concentrates on developing your powers of intuition rather than relying on expensive clairvoyants to choose your path for you.

Once you have learned one system, it is very easy to move on to the other forms of divination described in these books.

Rune Divination for Today's Woman

Many women don't use runes because they seem complicated. But by drawing simple symbols on pebbles you can tap into a magic that is as fresh today as when Anglo-Saxon women first tried to juggle relationships and family with the need for finding their own identity.

Tarot Divination for Today's Woman

The ancient symbols of the Tarot can be adapted to the lives of women today, using a very simple spread to build up a picture of options available. For this is fortune-making, not fortune-telling and relies, not on some external magic, but your own very powerful intuitions.

Crystal Divination for Today's Woman

Crystals and semi-precious stones provide a very powerful form of divination by harnessing the energies of your own powerful inner magic. You don't need to be an expert geologist to use the system which is based on a very simple colour method which you can adapt to your own special needs.

I Ching Divination for Today's Woman

Take away the image of the male Chinese civil servant which, until now has dominated the I Ching and it reflects a woman's natural approach to magic and change. Using the more ancient system, based on the natural forces of fire, sky, water, earth, trees, thunder, mountains and lakes, women can interpret their own present and plan the future.

The book shows how to make simple I Ching pebbles to work out your trigrams in seconds.

Pendulum Divination for Today's Woman

Whether your pendulum is finest crystal or an old key on a piece of string, you can use it to dowse, not for oil or water, but for your future options and your present health. The system uses simple circle cloths to focus your natural intuitive wisdom and make sure that you stay in control of your own decision-making.

About the Author

Cassandra Eason is a mother of five children and lives on the Isle of Wight. She juggles writing and broadcasting with taking care of the family, and the vacuum cleaner with the word processor, and frequently ends up fusing both. From an ordinary home in the back streets of Birmingham, she won a scholarship to an exclusive school (her Dad's bike would be parked alongside the Rolls-Royces at Open Evenings).

She became a teacher and then married a nice middle-class boy but found out that nice china at tea-time wasn't the same as a warm heart. Cassandra was rescued from a tumbledown cottage in Cornwall with two small children by a middle-aged knight in a Renault 4 whom she later married. Together they had

three more children.

While the children were small, Cassandra trained in psychology with the idea of returning to teaching. But she was pushed into a writing career when her middle son, Jack, told her that his dad was falling off his motor bike as it was happening 40 miles away.

The response to this experience from ordinary mothers led to her first book, *The Psychic Power of Children* which looks at the extraordinary psychic experiences of ordinary people.

This has been re-published with many new cases by Foulsham, along with its companion volume, *Psychic Suburbia.*

Her interest in divination methods grew while she was researching these books. Since the publication of the *Today's Woman* series, she has appeared on radio and television demonstrating her methods.